Testimonials

'From our first meeting, I found Roxanne an easy person to connect with. She explained everything I needed to know, and when I had questions, she did not hesitate to answer them clearly, as I had never done anything like this before. It is a frightening experience for someone like me who has never had a book previously published. Roxanne was with me every step of the way, encouraging me to continue when all I wanted to do was throw in the towel. Some days I wanted to cry because it became overwhelming at times as I started to compare myself to other authors and worry that my book may not be good enough for the public to read.

Roxanne made sure I was always in control of the whole process and encouraged me to never give up. Roxanne has the ability to innately know what you need; she is invested in doing her best to make you the best. All I can say is she makes you feel like you are the only one she is helping because she is so focused on how you are coping and cares by sending emails or calling to see how you are and always replies quickly to any correspondence. I cannot thank Roxanne enough for all that she has done for me, and I am confident as an author to continue writing.'

Nita Jane, *author of The Ancient Words of Wisdom*

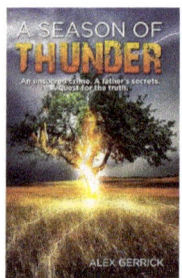 

'I struggled with my writing until I met Roxy. She immediately gave me a template and an identity to fulfill my talent, and her guidance has been invaluable. She also provided me with the confidence to break new boundaries and seek another level with my writing. Having her by my side every step of the way has made all the difference. She is a terrific mentor, and I am incredibly grateful for all her support. I could not have published two books, one of which has attracted much critical acclaim, without her guidance and advice. I look forward to working with her in future ventures.'

Alex Gerrick, *author of A Season of Clouds and A Season of Thunder*

'After losing my young husband to bowel cancer in early 2021, I had the idea to write down as much as I could remember for our son, Billy. What started as just a 'nice thought' and the intention to journal my thoughts, was transformed into the idea of a book after attending Roxanne's Ignite & Write workshop. In just one day the inspiration and directive Roxanne possessed helped guide my idea into something so much more meaningful and therapeutic.

'Roxanne abolished any doubts I had about publishing a book that exposed some of the deepest, darkest thoughts within my heart and soul. Roxanne continuously boosted my confidence and encouraged me to believe that my story was important.

Not only was this a book for my son and my own healing, but for all the people I may be able to help along the way by sharing my story. I can't thank her enough for her empathy, compassion, encouragement and incredible expertise in teaching people to write with true authenticity and integrity.'

Leah Polwarth, *author of Letters to Billy*

'Roxanne is truly one of a kind – a thoughtful and highly experienced coach, mentor, author and interviewer. Her curiosity and genuine care for others are always evident and her ever-present smile lights the way for those of us who have had the privilege to work with her. As someone who has benefited immensely from Roxanne's guidance, I can't express enough how much she has helped me bring my own book to life.

She has been my go-to person for any writing questions, providing invaluable feedback and support every step of the way. Her ability to help others get unstuck and navigate their journey to becoming authors is nothing short of remarkable. Thank you, Roxanne, for being such a positive force and for showing so many of us the path to sharing our stories with the world.'

Mukesh Bajaj, *author of 7 Steps to a Fulfilled Life*

'When I first considered writing *Talinga*, the story within me was vivid, but the path to bringing it to life felt overwhelming. I knew I needed a collaborator not only gifted with words, but also capable of understanding my vision and translating my thoughts into meaningful prose. That's when I decided to seek the assistance of a ghostwriter. From our very first conversation, Roxanne brought a sense of professionalism, empathy and genuine enthusiasm for the project. I was immediately reassured by her ability to listen deeply not just to the words I spoke, but to the intentions and emotions behind them.

She asked insightful questions, gently teased out the details that mattered and always showed a remarkable sensitivity to my voice. Over the ten months of working together, she became more than just a writer for hire; she was a confidante and creative partner. There were moments when I doubted myself or struggled to articulate complex memories, but she always responded with patience, encouragement and understanding. Her thoughtful approach made the writing process not just productive but deeply fulfilling. I never felt rushed or unheard.

Her meticulous attention to detail, ability to organise my scattered thoughts, and talent for crafting compelling narratives were invaluable. But even more meaningful was the trust and camaraderie that developed between us. She honoured my story as if it were her own, respecting its nuances while gently guiding the manuscript toward clarity and coherence.

When *Talinga* was finally published, I felt a profound sense of achievement and gratitude. I could see myself reflected in every page, but I also recognised the subtle artistry of my ghostwriter in the steady hand that shaped my recollections into a book I am truly proud of. To anyone considering a ghostwriter, I cannot recommend Roxanne enough. She transformed the daunting task of writing a book into a journey of discovery, healing, and creative joy. For that, and her unwavering support, I am deeply thankful.'

Margaret Sinclair, *author of Talinga: The house my dad built and its role in saving K'gari*

'Roxanne contributed to my book, *How to Become Your Best Version: Wisdom Shared by the Women of the Becoming Your Best Version Podcast.* She is a font of helpful wisdom for women seeking to express their authentic selves and get their stories out into the world. I am fortunate to have been one of the women with whom she shared her considerable gifts!'

Maria Leonard Olsen, *attorney, podcaster, TEDx speaker, author of 50 After 50: Reframing the Next Chapter of Your Life and How to Become Your Best Version*

'When my original publisher went bankrupt, my world tumbled down before me. I had lost not just money but my access to my manuscript, my thoughts and beliefs. Roxanne was recommended to me, and what a blessing that was. So sympathetic to the situation, professional and helpful. I not only trusted her ability to edit and publish my book, but I felt I had found a friend. Now in my hand, I have a book I am very proud of. Thank you Roxanne and the Ignite & Write Publishing team for your guidance in getting my book to such a standard that I feel able to show and share it with others.'

Jan Wills Collins, *author of The Silent Intruder*

IGNITE & WRITE

BOOK THREE

The Published Author

Roxanne McCarty-O'Kane

Ignite & Write: The Published Author
© Roxanne McCarty-O'Kane 2025

www.roxannewriter.com
hello@roxannewriter.com.au

Facebook: facebook.com/roxannewriter
Instagram: @roxannewriter
LinkedIn: linkedin.com/in/roxannemccartyokane/

ABN: 62660117725

This book is sold with the understanding that the author is not offering specific, personal advice to the reader. By reading this book, you acknowledge and accept that book writing is a dynamic field, and no one-size-fits-all solution exists. It is your responsibility to evaluate the relevance and applicability of the advice provided in the context of your unique story vision.

For professional personalised advice about your book, get in touch with Roxanne directly. The author disclaims any responsibility for liability, loss or risk, personal or otherwise, arising as a consequence of the use and application of any of the contents of this book.

The information in this publication is provided for general purposes only. It is not to be relied on as a substitute for legal advice. You should at all times consult with your own lawyer, especially if your writing concerns matter before the court or for any issues regarding possible defamation.

All rights reserved. This book may not be reproduced in whole or in part, stored, posted on the internet, or transmitted in any form or by any means, electronic or mechanical, or by photocopying, recording, sharing or other means, without written permission from the author of this book. All content found online or offline without written permission is in breach of copyright law and, therefore, renders you liable for damages and at risk of prosecution.

Cover illustration by Cara Ord, www.caraordcreate.com
Published by Ignite & Write Publishing, www.igniteandwritepublishing.com

ISBN: 978-0-6455447-2-5 (paperback)

978-0-6455447-3-2 (ebook)

 A catalogue record for this book is available from the National Library of Australia

May you remember that your voice matters, your story is powerful and the world needs what only you can give. Keep going, you are almost there!

Contents

A note from Roxy	1
Publishing process	9
Editing	15
Locking in your book's title	21
Internal design	25
Cover design	30
ISBN	42
Publishing avenues	45
Traditional/trade	49
Self-publishing	59
Independent	64
Product platforms	85
Offset printing	87
Print on demand	90
Ebooks	94
Audiobooks	98
Distribution	105
Marketing	111
Grow an audience	114
Leverage your audience	128
Website	142
Media	152

Launching	161
Pricing your book	163
Planning the event	168
The bestseller	185
Pre-sales	187
The pep talk	195
Acknowledgments	199
About Roxy	203
References	207
The Ignite & Write Trilogy	210

A note from Roxy

Hey there!

I see you. You're standing on the edge of something really big and I couldn't be more thrilled to be your chauffeur for this part of the authorship ride. The publishing phase is where your dreams become tangible. It's where the vision in your mind becomes something readers can actually touch, see, hear and be moved by.

Regardless of whether have already finished your manuscript and are ready to launch into editing right now, or you are the type of person who needs to know all the information before diving in boots and all, there is one thing aspiring authors all have in common – they get butterflies when they think about holding that completed book in their hands (and maybe even sniffing the pages… we all do it). If that's you, congratulations! You're in exactly the right place.

If you're joining me for the first time, welcome! I'm Roxanne McCarty-O'Kane, a professional ghostwriter, book coach and founder of the award-winning business Ignite & Write, which supports authors like you who have powerful stories from first page to publication. I've spent years walking alongside first-time and seasoned authors, helping them craft powerful nonfiction stories that connect deeply with their readers and position them as experts in their field.

I've also now published three of my own books, the first of which earned an international book award and became the spark for the publishing service provider arm of the business. If you've been with me since book one, hi again, and feel free to skim the next few paragraphs (you probably know me better than I know myself by now!).

For the longest time, I didn't believe I had a story worth sharing. It was just my ordinary life, nothing groundbreaking. But hindsight is a beautiful thing. I now see how every chapter, every setback and every moment of doubt shaped the storyteller I've become today. From curling up with books to escape small-town New Zealand life, to navigating the sting of rejection when a childhood dream of joining the Australian Defence Force slipped through my fingers, the throughline has always been words. They were my refuge then, and they're my purpose now.

My journey into storytelling through books wasn't linear. It took shape through unpaid internships at local newspapers and eventually, ink-stained fingers from community newsrooms where I was trusted to write, edit, photograph and connect with people whose stories deserved to be told. After more than a decade as a journalist and editor covering everything from celebrities to community champions, I found myself unexpectedly made redundant. That door closing opened another: ghostwriting.

A note from Roxy

The shift came after a powerful business conference where I realised that every speaker on stage had written a book, and I had the perfect blend of experience, empathy and word-nerdery to help others do the same.

Today, I'm proud to say I've ghostwritten dozens of nonfiction titles, in addition to publishing my own books. Ghostwriting gives me the chance to walk beside incredible changemakers and amplify their voices. But for those of you who feel called to write your story in your own words, I'm here too – to guide, cheerlead and gently nudge you over the finish line when the self-doubt creeps in.

I share all of this with you not for the spotlight, but to show you what's possible and to model the power of connection, which is at the core of everything I do. I could have simply listed my qualifications and awards, but that wouldn't have given you a sense of who I am or *why* I do this work. Stories build trust, create resonance and move people. That's exactly what your story has the power to do. So whether you're self-publishing, pitching to a traditional publisher, or not quite sure yet, know that you are not alone.

Now here's the thing no one tells you loud enough: becoming a published author brings up all the feelings.

Ignite & Write: The Published Author

Sure, there's the excitement and thrill of seeing your name in print, the rush of people reading your words. But there's also fear. The fear of being seen. The fear of being judged. The fear of getting it 'wrong'. I want you to know that's *completely normal*. You're not broken, you're brave! Because stepping into the role of a published author isn't just a professional milestone, it's the culmination of a personal transformation. It's a declaration to the world that your story, your knowledge, your truth *matters*.

The road to publishing is rarely straight. There's no universal blueprint, no perfect order of steps. Publishing is a 'choose your own adventure' kind of journey. And that's why this book won't give you a strict step-by-step formula. Instead, it's your behind-the-scenes pass to understanding your options, making informed decisions and confidently choosing the path that aligns with your goals, values and capacity. It will allow you to pave a path of purpose.

When I was preparing to publish my first book, I already had experience supporting authors behind the scenes at a hybrid publisher. I understood the process, but I also knew I didn't have time to learn every single skill needed to do it solo. So, I took the indie route, engaging a publishing service provider to support me. The result was an uplifting and empowering experience that left me standing taller as an author. For my second book, I wanted more control and more connection, so I built my own A-team: an editor with decades of experience and a designer who had co-founded one of Australia's first self-publishing companies. That launch? It was a dream, and it marked the moment Ignite & Write officially became a publishing services provider. I don't just teach this, I *live* it.

A note from Roxy

Because I've been where you are, I know how overwhelming it can be when everyone has a different opinion about 'the best' way to publish. People will always speak from their own experiences; some who have felt frustrated by traditional publishing's slow timelines and tight control, and others who've self-published but found the DIY route exhausting. The truth is, there is no best way; there is only *your* way. This book exists to help you find it.

We're going to talk about all the options from self-publishing to traditional publishing and everything in between. We'll look at what's involved, what to expect and how to protect your creative energy (and sanity) along the way. We will also delve into how to market and sell your book, which is the oft-forgotten but most important phase for any author. After all, what good is putting in all the time and effort if your book remains the best-kept secret?

But before we get too deep into logistics, I want to take you back to your 'why'. Remember that powerful question I asked you way back in *The Mindful Author*? If you've written it down and pinned it to your wall, go look at it now. If it's lost under a pile of notebooks, don't worry, this is your invitation to revisit it. Or, better yet, head back to my first book and complete the Five Why Technique with a slightly new version: *Why do I want to publish my work?* [1]

Understanding the deep-rooted reason behind your desire to publish is one of the most powerful tools an author can harness. Your 'why' acts as your internal compass, guiding every decision you make on the publishing journey from the publishing avenue to the format and distribution channels. Without clarity on this core motivation, it's easy to get swayed by trends or overwhelmed by options. But when your 'why' is crystal clear, every step from structuring your manuscript to selecting between traditional, independent, or self-publishing becomes a strategic move that aligns with your bigger vision.

Let that be your compass as we go forward because, at the end of the day, your book is more than just a product. It's a reflection of you. So, let's honour it and give it the launch it deserves.

Roxanne McCarty-O'Kane

A note from Roxy

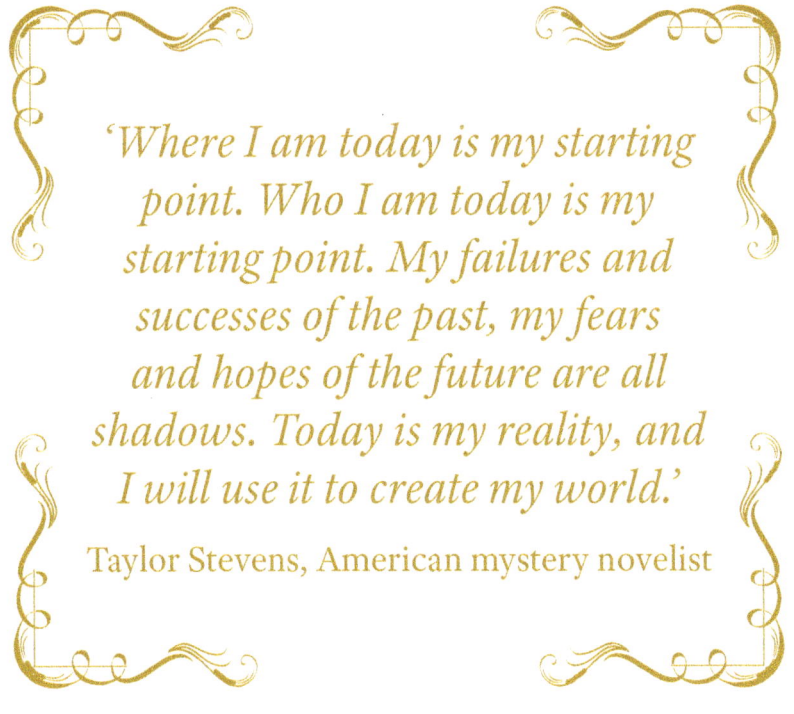

'Where I am today is my starting point. Who I am today is my starting point. My failures and successes of the past, my fears and hopes of the future are all shadows. Today is my reality, and I will use it to create my world.'

Taylor Stevens, American mystery novelist

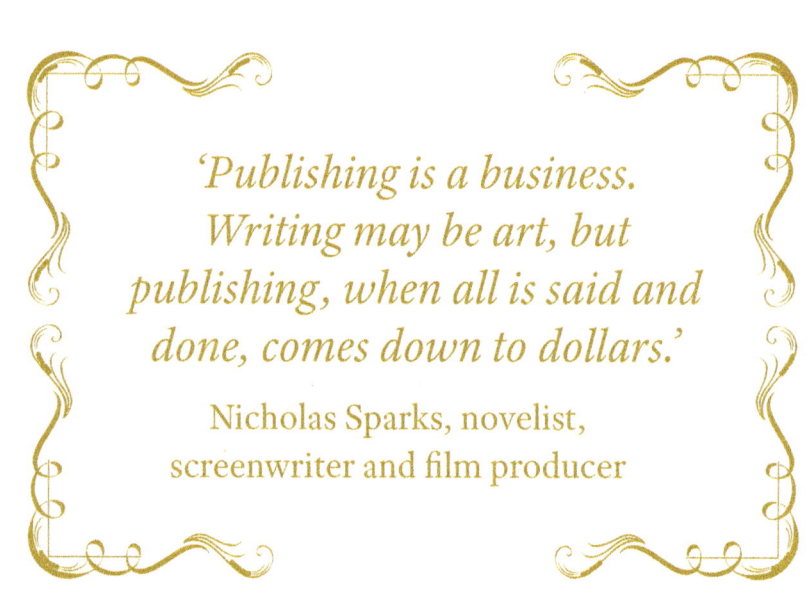

'Publishing is a business. Writing may be art, but publishing, when all is said and done, comes down to dollars.'

Nicholas Sparks, novelist, screenwriter and film producer

Publishing process

Google estimated that by August 2010, there had been 129,864,880 books published throughout human history.² Fast forward just over a decade and, as of 2022, that number had risen to 156,264,880 titles.³ But here's the kicker – this number only accounts for books with official ISBNs. It doesn't include the exploding world of ebooks, audiobooks, or independently published titles that never make it into the traditional catalogues.

If we factored those in, the number would be astronomical. According to UNESCO, around 2.2 million new titles are added to the global bookshelf every single year.⁴

Let that settle in for a moment.

I don't share these numbers to overwhelm you; quite the opposite. I want to ground you in the reality of the publishing landscape. This isn't to say your book will be lost in the crowd. It's to highlight just how important it is to approach this journey with clarity, purpose and structure. It's the difference between simply publishing a book and publishing a book that makes an impact.

> You don't need to be one in 156 million, you just need to be the one your reader has been waiting for.

This chapter is your roadmap through the publishing process. Whether you're planning to go the traditional route, tap into independent options, or self-publish entirely on your own terms,

Publishing process

it's essential to understand how the machine works so you can make informed decisions.

But before we dive in, let's take a moment to talk about expectations. Many first-time authors dream of becoming the next big thing, selling a million copies, landing on international bestseller lists and being interviewed on morning TV shows. While I'll never tell you not to dream big (you know I'm all for bold vision!), I *will* encourage you to connect deeply with your real motivation for writing and publishing your book.

Do you want to:

- Position yourself as a thought leader?
- Share a message that changes lives?
- Support your business or career?
- Honour your story and create a legacy?

You may have a single purpose or a combination of them. Considering these questions from each point of view – first writing, then publishing – means a varied approach. Like with your writing, these decisions will guide your path when it comes to producing a tangible book. This is the reason I always challenge authors to understand their 'why.' It is the first, and arguably most important, step in this journey.

Barry Bull is a former musician and national record company executive best known for his multi-award-winning Brisbane business Toombul Music, which he kept in the spotlight of the Australian music industry for more than twenty-five years. Barry had four business books – *A Little Bull Goes a Long Way*,

Ignite & Write: The Published Author

My Little Book of Bull, *The Bullseye Principle*, *Take the Bull by the Horns* – two of which were traditionally published and the other two self-published. But as he shared with the *Ignite & Write Podcast* (formerly known as *The Phoenix Phenomenon Podcast* – a bit of a mouthful!), when it came to his fifth book, *UnbreakaBULL*, his 'why' lent itself to self-publishing because he wanted to have full control, as the story was based around his relationship with his late wife.

> 'I didn't want this to be a commercial project because this was a love story and it was really done as narrative therapy for me. So, when people tell me they're enjoying my book, I qualify that by saying, 'Well, I didn't really write it for anybody else but myself and it helped me get through this awful journey of grief'. I approached it as a non-commercial project and I wanted to self-publish because I... decided to be in control of it myself rather than assign copyrights and properties to other people. It was really a project that was very personal to me to talk about our life together, and you know what, it just turned out so much better than I ever thought it would because I had freedom to self-express... and it really just helped me mend a broken heart.'

You can watch the full interview here:

Publishing process

In the pages ahead, I'll walk you through the publishing process so you can navigate each stage with confidence, avoid common pitfalls and create a book that not only meets the industry's standards but also fulfils your unique purpose.

IN THE KNOW: KEY PUBLISHING ELEMENTS

It can take several months from the time you have written your shitty first draft (SFD), reviewed it and made amendments to create your second draft. Whether you will be responsible for the various steps or not will depend on the publishing path you choose. You'll understand this concept better once you tackle that chapter. You will either have these steps taken care of for you, engage a professional to carry them out, or do them yourself.

The publishing process has several steps. When you take a bird's-eye view, it looks a little something like this:

 If you haven't had any professional guidance while writing your book, once you have refined your SFD using the self-editing tips from *The Structured Author*, I recommend engaging a professional editor for a structural edit to double-check the overall flow of your manuscript.

 Implement the editor's recommendations that you agree with to create a third draft.

- Copy editing comes next. This is where the editor looks through the microscope at sentence structure, grammar, facts and spelling.
- Proofreading. The final net to catch any lingering typos that may have slipped through the cracks up until that point.
- Internal design, also known as formatting or typesetting, follows. This is where you choose the size and style of your book.
- Next, lock in your book title.
- Your designer will work on the cover, creating a front, back and spine that is engaging for your ideal reader.
- Register the ISBN (International Standard Book Number), which becomes the barcode for your book.
- Choose whether you would like to bulk-print physical books, utilise print on demand (POD), release an ebook, record an audiobook or any combination of these.
- Marketing, marketing, marketing!

Because knowledge is power in the world of publishing, and you are likely feeling a little overwhelmed by the process, I'll break each of these steps down into further detail so you know what to

Publishing process

expect and how it all works. After all, when you are confident in what you are doing, you are more likely to have a fun publishing experience, which is what I'm all about!

Editing

You might not realise it, but your brain is a code-cracking machine.

For emaxlpe, it deson't mttaer in waht oredr the ltteers in a wrod aepapr, the olny iprmoatnt tihng is taht the frist and lsat ltteer are in the rghit pcale. The rset can be a toatl mses and you can sitll raed it wouthit pobelrm.

S1M1L4RLY, Y0UR M1ND 15 R34D1NG 7H15 4U70M471C4LLY W17H0U7 3V3N 7H1NK1NG 4B0U7 17.

Passages like the above have been blowing people's minds on the internet for decades, but it is important to consider just how easy it is for our minds to 'fill in the blanks.' This ability increases tenfold when you are the author of words that may be jumbled up on the page. When you consider that the average book has around seventy thousand words in it, there's no doubt that there are numerous errors buried within, no matter how careful you have been.

The phenomenon that allows most people to read the paragraphs above easily has been given the slightly tongue-in-cheek name typoglycemia, and it works because our brains don't just rely on what they see – they also rely on what we *expect* to see.[5]

In 2011, researchers from the University of Glasgow, conducting unrelated research, found that when something is obscured from or unclear to the eye, human minds can predict what they think they're going to see and fill in the blanks.[6]

You can understand then, why it is so important to engage a third party to support you with editing your book. An editor will catch spelling errors, misplaced or misused words more easily because they are experiencing your work for the first time and literally don't know what's coming next.

They can also identify gaps in your storytelling. When writing your manuscript, you will know something was said or done because you lived it, but you may not have actually written it down. Instead, your mind fills that in, while a fresh reader would miss it entirely because it does not exist. This can create unexplained gaps in your narrative flow that are jarring for your reader.

The magic of fresh eyes should never be underestimated.

If you want to create a professional book, editing is the largest financial investment piece when you are self or indie publishing, but there is a good reason for that. Software programs and AI can only do so much. They can rarely catch the difference between the application of similar words like 'form' and 'from' if they are used in the incorrect context but spelled correctly. They also do not have the ability to recognise the use of punctuation that can add emphasis and impact to language for a reader.

Publishing process

This is why human editors remain far superior to any electronic options and should never be undervalued. I know there have been many times where I've been deeply enthralled and engaged in a particular book, and then I'll come across a spelling error or perhaps there's a misplaced word or word missing completely, and it just jars you out of the world you had been invested in. Errors, whether structural or grammatical, interfere with the reading experience.

Maybe it happens more to me because I'm sensitive to errors, given my background in print media and books being my area of expertise, but one thing I know for sure is that when your readers experience that multiple times while reading your book, it is not a good look, particularly if you want to use your book for your business or to establish yourself as a credible expert.

In the glory days of print media, we had journalists who reported and wrote, while the sub-editors corrected the work of the writers. The rule of thumb was that you never edited your own work, and I believe this is absolutely crucial when it comes to writing books as well.

There is obvious temptation for you to think you can save a few bucks by just editing a manuscript yourself (or asking your sister-in-law to edit it for you because she is an English teacher), but as explained, we have this innate ability to switch on our own autocorrect. You've spent a great deal of time writing and refining your manuscript, you know exactly what you want to say and where your sentences and paragraphs lead, and if there are some mistakes, that autocorrect kicks in, and you will miss it.

The power of having a professional editor step in is that they have fresh eyes. They don't know essentially where your book is going; they don't have that anticipation of what the next word should be; they're coming at it from a completely clear space with skilled expertise, and they, for that reason, will pick up on those little mistakes. I know, it can be frustrating to see how many errors they find, but look at it as a win – for every error they correct, you are paving the way for a seamless reader experience.

I also know how hard it can be to hand over your book baby to someone you may never have met before and let them work on it. But trust that if you engage a professional who knows what they are doing, you will be in safe hands.

Through Ignite & Write, we cover four levels of editing:

1. Developmental assessment

Even the best in the biz don't publish a first draft! So, if you have placed the final full stop on your manuscript and are looking for professional feedback on how to improve it, this is the step for you.

A developmental edit is a big-picture look at the overall flow and structure of your book, and includes a number of steps.

- Identifying if themes are properly explored and developed.
- Establishing if 'characters' pop in without context or purpose.

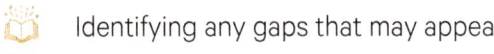

Publishing process

- Identifying any gaps that may appear in timelines.
- The balance of lengthy versus short chapters and if they may need to be adjusted.
- Assessing the chapter hierarchy, including parts, main chapters and the use of subheadings and other structural elements.
- Whether more clarity or context is needed to explain an event or educational point in your book.
- Highlighting areas that may be danger zones for copyright infringement or potential defamation (please note, we are not lawyers, but we can definitely identify red flags for you).
- Whether there is relevance to and an appropriate connection for your ideal reader or target market.

All of these observations (and more) are compiled into a document along with suggestions on how you can weave in the necessary improvements. You can then work on implementing those changes to create your second draft.

2. Structural edit

A structural edit is similar to a developmental edit in that it examines the overall presentation of your book. But there is one key difference – it is more intensive, and we make the changes for you.

We will then connect with you to run through our suggested changes and, with your approval, will go ahead and execute those changes, leaving you free to focus on other important things in your life.

3. Copy/line edit

Once your manuscript is structurally sound, this is where we get down to the nitty-gritty.

When the copy/line edit is complete, you will have a manuscript that is ready to be designed and transformed into a book! The editor will literally go through your manuscript line by line with a fine-tooth comb to ensure that:

- style is consistent
- spelling suits your audience (AUS/UK/US English)
- spelling errors are corrected
- names of people and places are correct and consistent
- punctuation usage is correct
- grammar is tidied up
- typos or misused words are corrected
- fact boxes and pull quote style is uniform
- sentences are clear and concise
- tone of voice is consistent
- tenses are clear and utilised properly
- repetitive text is removed or reworded.

Publishing process

4. Proofread

This is the last stop in the editing phase. Depending on your publisher, this step can be done either before or after the manuscript is typeset (designed).

It is an important step because it catches the things that may have been missed in the copy edit. Believe me, it is rare to find a book without a single error but having a proofread as part of your manuscript preparation process means the book is as 'clean' as possible.

Locking in your book's title

Choosing a book title can feel like trying to name a child because it's personal, meaningful and needs to stand the test of time. I have worked with authors who have known their book title before they had even written the first word of their shitty first draft and others who are still scrambling to settle on something when the designer is patiently waiting.

Your title doesn't have to come to you in a lightning bolt of inspiration, so don't despair if it hasn't arrived unexpectedly in your mind in the middle of the night. Instead, think of it as a strategic tool to help your book find the right readers. A good title should give a clear sense of what the book is about, who it's for and why someone should pick it up. Clarity beats cleverness, especially in nonfiction, where the reader is often seeking transformation or insight.

One of the most helpful rules is to use your 'why' as a compass. Often, this holds the gold because it spells out the promise or purpose of your book. Once you know what you're delivering, you can pair it with a main title that evokes emotion, curiosity, or relevance. For example, if your 'why' is to show people how to reset their relationship with food and become healthier, your title could be something like, *Eat Like You Love Yourself,* which is emotive, memorable and aligned with your core message.

It is easy to get carried away in symbolism; it is something I was guilty of early in my career. I loved the symbolism of the phoenix and how it related to the transformation authors go through when they convert their past experiences of loss, hurt and trauma into words on the page that have the power to change lives. And so, I was set firmly on calling my writing program *The Phoenix Phenomenon*. Sure, it sounded fancy, and it allowed me to sit in my creative brilliance, but anyone coming across it would have absolutely no idea what it meant!

Any title that requires an explanation can tap into a subtitle to enhance clarity for your potential readers, but if you can find a way to pair a powerful (and easily understood) title with a qualifying subtitle, you have the power combo.

This has been the realisation a few of my authors have had during their own journeys. Stew Darling's *Lead through Life* was initially going to be called *Blue Sand*. He had wanted that name because it reflected the blue of his military uniform and captured the sandy landscape of the Middle East, where he served. It was too abstract for his readers, who needed to know what they would get from this leadership book. So, he went back to basics and found a powerful title that left no grey areas.

Don't be afraid to test your title ideas. Try them out loud. Share them in conversations. Ask your community for feedback. A title should be easy to say, easy to spell and easy to remember. If people consistently mispronounce it, forget it, or ask what it means, it might not be working. Also, do a quick search on Amazon or Google Books. If there are ten other books with the same title in your genre, consider tweaking yours to stand out.

One thing to note is that you cannot trademark or copyright a book title.

This is a huge bugbear for some authors, but it is an unavoidable truth. There may already be other books with the same title as yours, and if you love it so much that you can't let it go, this is where a well-crafted subtitle will come to your rescue.

 Subtitle

A strong title might catch a reader's eye, but it's often the subtitle or tagline that seals the deal because it provides a succinct explanation. It should work with the title, not compete with it.

A subtitle or tagline is particularly important in nonfiction, where readers want to know exactly what they're getting. Take, for example, *Atomic Habits* by James Clear. The title is punchy and memorable, but without the subtitle, the purpose of the book is unclear. While the word 'habits' is pretty self-explanatory, we do not know if they are good habits or bad habits. 'Atomic' is open to even more interpretation. It could mean:

- a scientific theory and focus on energy, atoms or chemistry
- a metaphor for something with explosive power
- something tiny, as in the size of an atom, such as habits that are small actions that can create a larger, cumulative outcome.

Because James included the subtitle, 'An easy & proven way to build good habits & break bad ones,' all the grey disappears and the reader knows exactly what they are getting themselves into.

Keep these things in mind when crafting your subtitle:

- The fewer words, the better. A lengthy paragraph is going to clog up your front cover design.
- A great subtitle quickly answers the question every potential reader is silently asking: *What's in it for me?*
- If your title is a little abstract, your subtitle needs to anchor the clarity.
- When it comes to design, the main title should always be larger and bolder than the subtitle.
- Ensure your subtitle matches the tone of your book. A memoir or business book requires a snappy, direct subtitle that could incorporate humour, whereas a spiritual book would require more poetic language.

Publishing process

Internal design

Once your manuscript is complete and edited, it's time to transform your words into a *book*. This is where the internal designer steps in. These professionals can also be known as book formatters, layout designers or typesetters, and they are responsible for how your book looks on the inside – from the title page to the final full stop.

A good format designer doesn't just insert your words into a template; they shape the reading experience by creating a seamless design that doesn't distract from the work you have created.

You may have a clear idea of what style of font you prefer or how you want your pages laid out, but it is perfectly fine if you don't. For some first-time authors, trying to figure out what serif and sans serif actually mean does nothing but give them a headache! This is where it is important to have an experienced designer in your corner.

Formatters choose fonts that match the tone of your content, determine the spacing and margins, design chapter headings and ensure consistency across every page.

IN THE KNOW: A GUIDE TO FONTS

Whether your book is a memoir, a business how-to or a self-help guide, your format designer makes it readable, professional and polished. You can give them a head start just by understanding whether you like serif or sans serif fonts.

If it sounds like I'm speaking another language, I completely understand. There are so many nuances to text that we don't even think about as readers.

 Serif fonts have small decorative strokes or 'feet' at the ends of each letter. These little lines or embellishments help guide the reader's eye along lines of text, which is why serif fonts are traditionally used in printed books. Common serif fonts include:

- Times New Roman
- Georgia
- Garamond
- Baskerville

 Sans serif fonts are clean and modern-looking, with no extra strokes at the ends of the letters. *Sans* literally means 'without' in French, so sans serif means without the serifs. These fonts are commonly used in digital formats, like websites, apps and social media, because they're crisp

Publishing process

and clear on screens, but they are becoming more popular in published books (like this one!) Common sans serif fonts include:

- **Arial**
- Calibre (the font used in this book)
- Century Gothic
- **Verdana**

There are more fonts out there than you can poke a stick at. If you want your mind to be truly blown, visit 1001fonts.com. But I would advise that you listen to the expertise of your designer when it comes to making the final selection. If you are anything like me, you might have thought a beautiful, flowy cursive font is what you need, but when you see it on the page, chances are, it will be difficult to read.

In print books, design affects aspects such as page count and visual flow. In ebooks, it affects navigation and accessibility. An unformatted or poorly formatted book can confuse or even frustrate your readers. A well-formatted book, on the other hand, lets your message shine without distraction.

If you have graphic design or similar experience, you can absolutely DIY, but please be aware there are definite nuances to book design that need to be understood. Book formatters have a deep understanding of book production processes, typography and layout, while graphic designers focus on creating visual concepts for different media.

Ignite & Write: The Published Author

An experienced formatter will be able to guide you through the many choices that need to be made for your book design, but you can start to consider these components to get ahead and make your interactions smoother.

- Make sure your manuscript is fully edited and proofread. Designers work from the final version, not a work in progress.

- Do you want a paperback, hardcover, ebook, or all three? Each platform has specific formatting specs, so once your designer knows your vision, they can ensure that each of those is met.

- For physical books, do you have a preferred trim size? This is the physical size of the book and the dimensions refer to the length and width of the cover. The most common size for non-fiction books is 6"x9" (15.24 x 22.86 centimetres), however, other common trim sizes include 5.5"x 8.5", 5"x7" and 4.25" x 6.87".

- Share your genre and ideal reader with your design, as this can influence design style. The aesthetic of a workbook is different to a memoir!

- Check out other books in your genre and show your designer examples of designs you really like the look and feel of. You can also bring in examples of things you do not like because that can be just as powerful for your designer.

- Any specific fonts you love or hate? Do you have a font that you use across all of your branding that you would like to have incorporated? Designers appreciate guidance, but readability will be the final deciding factor in the end.

- Are there elements like quotes, exercises, tips or illustrations that appear regularly? These often need special treatment in the layout.
- Will your book include photos, charts or diagrams? Make sure these are high resolution and labelled clearly. I recommend setting up a folder in the cloud that you can easily share with your designer. The easier you can make it for the designer to find the right elements for the right page, the better. Consider:
  - renaming your photos as the captions you would like to appear in the book
  - organising your photos into a folder for each chapter
  - including a low-resolution version of the photo in the manuscript if you would like them designed in place on the page rather than as a collection in the middle of the book.

Internal design can be used strategically.

For example, if you have a smaller number of words (such as twenty thousand to forty thousand words), you can consider a smaller book size to boost the number of pages. You can also tap into creative elements like font size, pull quotes and boxed areas that produce white space and simultaneously boost page count.

If you have a higher word count and want to minimise the number of pages, it can be a little trickier. But a great designer will be able to work with a font size that is still accessible for the majority of readers and work with other elements, like line spacing, to pack as much in as possible while still looking fabulous.

Make sure you are aware of the level of support your designer will provide for you. Do they offer design mock-ups for a chapter or two so you can get a visual before they apply the design to the whole manuscript? Also check if those mock-ups will give you multiple options to choose from. This is invaluable for people like me who don't often know what they want until they physically see it on the page. From there, I can easily pick what I like and don't like. Also, check how many revisions of the design are included in their fees.

Cover design

The old saying, 'don't judge a book by its cover', may be a wonderful lens through which to view situations and the people you come across in life, but ironically, it is absolutely incorrect for actual book covers!

When it comes to selling books, *every* potential reader judges a book by its cover. This is why I recommend that you don't think you can save money by pulling something together on free software platforms like Canva. During my time in print media, I learned that good design often goes unnoticed because it follows visual rules our eyes naturally appreciate. Bad design, however, is instantly obvious when those rules are ignored.

Publishing process

It is one thing to know the rules and be rebellious in how you break them, but it is another thing entirely when you believe they don't apply to you. I belong to dozens of author groups and I can tell in one-millionth of a second when a cover has been created by an amateur wanting to save some coin. No, I won't even use the word 'designed'.

While saving money on design fees may seem appealing at first, it ultimately reduces the chances that potential readers, who are unfamiliar with you and your work, will find your book worth their time. It may sound harsh, but I like to be honest about these things.

Picture this: you are standing in a bookshop, facing two books on the same topic. One has a clear font, a well-thought-out composition, colours that are contemporary and complementary and imagery that evokes the theme of the book. The other has a cursive font that is hard to read, a subtitle that runs over four lines, no author name and a clip art-style graphic reminiscent of those available in early versions of Microsoft Word. I know which book I would choose.

Now, that's an extreme example, but if you scroll through any subject listing on Amazon, I can guarantee that you will come across a number of obvious homemade cover thumbnails... but they will never be in the first couple of pages. They will be buried far, far back in the catalogue because they are not getting any traction.

In addition, because aesthetics play a huge role in how marketable your book is, independent bookstores will be far less inclined to put your book on their shelves if it does not meet the industry standards.

So, what are the characteristics of good book cover design?

 Your genre is clear

You want the reader to look at your cover and clearly identify your book's genre. Next time you are in a bookshop, spend some time comparing romance or crime novel covers with those in the autobiography or self-help section. You will see they greatly differ in appearance.

I must confess, my trilogy bucks the trend when it comes to this rule. The author support service I worked with on my first book was adamant that I have a white background instead of the black because the darker colour pushed my aesthetic into the realm of fantasy due to my use of the phoenix. But my vision (and branding) was the black, gold and fire colour palette, so I resisted. To be fair, I looked at both options, and it was a close call. I even market-tested covers and ultimately decided to go with my gut. I am proud that my book stands out a mile from other books on how to write because it does *not* have a white background.

 Readable fonts

The title must be easy to read, even in thumbnail size. Many people are purchasing their books online, and if they cannot easily see the title of your book, they will move on. Even if every other component of the cover design is sound, the font can make or break the overall look. If you already have branding, align your fonts to match this to build on brand recognition, but if not, steer clear of the 'fancy' fonts in favour of those that can be read by people from all walks of life. Simple typefaces often work best.

 Visual hierarchy

Design elements like the title, subtitle, author name and imagery should be arranged to guide the viewer's eye naturally. The title should take priority and be given the largest amount of real estate, followed by the subtitle and author. Select photos or graphics with the aim of enhancing the words rather than competing for attention with them.

 Ideal reader appeal

You've known who your ideal reader is since you picked up *The Mindful Author*, so this is the perfect opportunity to create something they will love. Consider their age, interests, colours that they would love, as well as design styles that would make them reach for your book. Yes, this is an exercise in marketing, but it is all valuable practice for the not-too-distant future when you will launch your book to your ideal readers.

If the designer you are working with allows you a couple of options to consider, you might like to pop them up for feedback. I tried this to aid with my black or white background dilemma and ended up with a 60/40 split in favour of black. It was validation that my ideal readers would still love to pick up my book even if it didn't fit the traditional style conventions.

Cohesive colour palette

If you love a splash of colour like me, you may be tempted to make it as bright and colourful as possible. I mean, you want it to pop off the shelf, right literally? Because there is only a limited amount of space on your cover, there is such a thing as too much when it comes to colour choice. If you can stick to a colour palette that evokes the right emotion and tone for the book and use two to three dominant colours at most, you won't overwhelm your reader.

 Designed for format

If you have decided to release both paperback and hardcover versions of your book, please note that this will require two separate designs because there are different dimensions at play. While they may have the same makeup visually, there are nuances to each format that require different sizing and other considerations. For example, with a paperback, you can have what is called a 'duplex', which is double-sided cover pages. This will require a different design file to a standard paperback cover.

Also, hardcovers can come in a variety of options, such as a printed case, where the design is placed directly onto the cover, or you can have a 'dust jacket,' which is the glossy additional wrap on top of the hardcover that can be removed. The options available to you will be determined by your chosen printing route, which you will learn more about later in this book.

Publishing process

 Professional imagery or illustration

I used the clip art example for shock factor before, but there are some out there who think it is okay to use basic graphics for their book covers. Please don't let that be you. Try to avoid stock photo clichés, not only because everyone else has access to the exact same photos as you if you choose from that pool, but it will place you in the world of 'ho hum,' and your cover will not be memorable.

There is also temptation to use AI-generated cover images, and while this is a rapidly evolving space, at the time of print, there were requirements to declare the use of AI when listing your book with online retailers. This can negatively impact the visibility of your book on online bookstores. It is also quite polarising and there are many readers who will turn away from a book with an AI cover because they assume the contents are also AI-derived and therefore inauthentic. Use high-quality, original illustrations, professionally taken photos (not something off your iPhone) or textures that enhance the story and give the cover a polished feel.

One of the most common questions I get from nonfiction authors is: 'Do I need to have a photo of myself on the cover?'

Let me reassure you right away, there is no hard-and-fast rule. But it *is* a strategic decision that depends on a few important factors.

Ignite & Write: The Published Author

- **What kind of book are you writing?**

    If your book is a memoir, a personal development guide, or deeply connected to your personal story, having a photo of yourself can work beautifully. It builds an instant sense of intimacy. The reader sees you and, whether they realise it or not, they start to form a connection. It says: *This is my story. I'm showing up, fully.*

    On the other hand, if you're writing business nonfiction, a how-to guide, or a topic-based book, your face might not be what draws the reader in. In these cases, your authority and the content take centre stage, so a bold title or graphic concept may be a better choice.

- **Are you the brand?**

    If your name is already a known entity because you are a speaker, coach or influencer with a strong personal brand, then featuring your photo can absolutely add weight. Your face *is* part of the marketing. But if you're just starting out, or if the book's message stands independently from your identity, there's no pressure to put your face front and centre.

- **What makes you feel comfortable?**

    This might sound like a 'soft' factor to consider, but it's actually one of the most important. Some authors *love* the idea of being the face of their book. Others squirm at the thought. If the idea of seeing your face on a bookstore shelf lights you up, go for it. If it makes you want to crawl under a table, don't force it. I believe there is energy attached to everything we do, and if you are not confident in standing on the top of a mountain, waving around a copy of your book with your face on the front, you will want to hide. That energy is not going to serve you well in getting your book out there.

If you *do* go with a photo, make sure it's professionally taken, well-lit and matches the mood of your book. No cropped selfies. No holiday snaps. No Zoom screenshots. The quality of your image sends a signal about the quality of your book. Also, let your photographer know they will need to build space into the composition for the title and other word components for your cover.

 Consistent branding

If you are launching into creating a series of books, think of how you can carry over design elements to create a cohesive collection. I knew from the moment I wrote *The Mindful Author* that I would write a series that stepped my ideal readers through from concept to completion with their books, so I had all three covers designed at the same time. This allowed me to see how they would look next to one another and play around with changing up different elements from the font to the colours and the phoenixes.

As you know, I ultimately chose to keep the same design across all three, with the only changes being the title of the book and the phoenix illustration. This way, the reader could see the progress of the phoenix emerging from the pages in book one, starting to shine and strengthen in book two and launching from the pages to be out in the world in book three. Symbolism works well when done correctly.

You only have to look at fiction writers who have amassed an impressive collection of work over the years to see how important structure and brand are when it comes to a book cover. Their fans can look at a cover and instantly recognise the author's work because they will use the same fonts, cover composition and imagery across all of their books. For you in the nonfiction world, this builds recognition and brand trust.

 Back cover and spine design

While attention to the front cover is important, don't neglect the spine and back cover for print books. The back cover should include a compelling blurb, barcode/ISBN and possibly an author photo (if you don't have yourself on the front).

When you look at the front, spine and back as a cohesive design, you can really elevate the experience for your readers. Take author Berni Morris-Smith's *The Griefcase,* for example. She had a captivating photo of herself sitting atop a mountain on the front cover, and the title had a cheeky briefcase in place of the dot on the 'i' (this is called a tittle, in case you were wondering). The spine and back cover were designed with a leather graphic to give it visual texture. The spine has a briefcase handle in the middle of it, so it looks like it is ready to be picked up and carried.

Publishing process

There are limitless ways you can adapt your cover design to create something unique for your subject matter that will connect even further with your ideal reader.

The words on your back cover essentially become the elevator pitch for your book. You've probably heard the term 'elevator pitch' in a business setting. Maybe you've had to introduce yourself in a networking group, on a Zoom call, or at a conference. If you've ever struggled to explain what you do in a way that's clear, compelling and brief, then you already know how tricky this can be.

Writing a back cover blurb is the same kind of challenge. The goal? To give your potential reader just enough to hook them without giving away the entire synopsis. You want to intrigue them so they will purchase your book and dive in for the full experience. Just like a powerful elevator pitch, a great back cover blurb needs a few key ingredients:

- Clarity – Say what the book is about in simple, specific terms. Don't be vague or clever for the sake of being clever. Being clear will always serve you well.
- Brevity – Keep it tight. You've got maybe one hundred and fifty to two hundred words at the most.
- Hook – Open with a bold statement, a relatable question, or a compelling insight. Think of your first sentence as your headline.
- Authenticity – Let your tone match your message. If your book is warm and inspiring, your blurb should feel the same. If it's bold and disruptive, don't write a blurb that sounds like a textbook.

IN THE KNOW: TIPS FOR WRITING YOUR BACK COVER BLURB

Unsure how to even start with a back cover blurb?

Grab a piece of paper and write down the who, what, when, where, why, and how of your book. Then craft a short paragraph that answers these questions:

- Who is this book for?
- What problem does it solve?
- Why did you write it?
- What promise are you making to the reader?
- How will their life/business/perspective be better after reading it?

Start with a bang! A grabbing statement or unique selling proposition (USP), if it is strong enough. Then finish with a question or an open-ended idea that makes the reader want to turn to the first page. Refine this until it is a maximum of 250 to 300 words.

What would your competitor do?

Before you fall in love with your own cover concept, take a moment to check out what is already out there in your genre. One of the smartest exercises in book cover design is to ask,

what would my competitor do? More specifically, *what have they done... and how is it working?*

Look at the bestselling books in your category. Study their covers like a designer, not just a reader. What colours are common? What fonts are frequently used? Is there a recurring visual theme? Are the covers minimalist or bold? Photographic or abstract?

This is not a copycat exercise; it is your chance to understand what is already out there, so you can do it better! There's no need to re-invent the wheel, so once you understand what is working, you can put your own spin on it. This is the delicate dance of cover design – standing out while fitting in.

If your book is too visually different, it risks being misunderstood or dismissed. If it's too similar, it might fade into the crowd. The sweet spot is a design that feels at home on the shelf but also invites a second look. Venture to your library or local bookstore and peruse.

I enjoy the cover creation process immensely when supporting authors like you through their publishing journey. That's because this is often the moment when you feel like your book is actually *real*. It is no longer just words on a computer screen; it is taking on its own personality and coming to life in a visual way. When you see your name on the bottom of the cover? Well, that is an indescribable buzz and brings with it a true sense of accomplishment. And guess what? That feeling is just around the corner for you!

ISBN

ISBN stands for International Standard Book Number, which sounds intimidating, but it's basically a fancy name for a book barcode.

This little string of digits plays a big role in getting your book into the hands of readers. It acts like your book's unique fingerprint because no two books (or editions of a book) share the same ISBN. It tells libraries, bookstores, distributors, online retailers and inventory systems that your book exists, what it's called, who published it and in the formats it is available in – all vital information for them to be able to order your book.

Here's what you need to know, depending on your chosen publishing path:

 If you're being traditionally or independently published, you can relax as you won't need to lift a finger. Your publisher or publishing support team will handle this behind the scenes as part of the production process. They'll register your ISBN, marry it to your book's metadata and ensure everything lines up in industry systems.

Traditional and hybrid publishers have their own ISBN prefixes, which are numbers that form part of the ISBN and indicate the publishing house. That's why, to a distributor or bookstore, the ISBN can subtly signal whether a book has come through a professional publishing process or whether it's been self-published.

Publishing process

Is this a dealbreaker? No. Many self-published books thrive. But if you're seeking wider distribution in bookstores or want to be taken seriously in certain markets, this perception may matter. Some authors choose to publish through platforms that offer ISBNs under a registered publishing imprint to avoid the 'self-pub stigma.' Others are proud to wear the self-published badge and simply ensure their production quality matches the trade publishing counterparts.

 If you're self-publishing, the responsibility for buying an ISBN lands in your lap. It's not hard, but it is important. In most countries, you'll need to go through your national ISBN agency (for example, Thorpe-Bowker in Australia, simply Bowker in the USA or Nielsen in the UK). Each ISBN typically comes with a fee, and you'll need a separate ISBN for every version of your book:

- paperback
- hardcover
- ebook
- audiobook.

Keep in mind that any future editions released with additional chapters will also require a new ISBN.

When you boil it down, your ISBN is just one of those behind-the-scenes elements that make your book legitimate, searchable and ready for real or virtual shelves. It's a small detail with a big impact.

'There is no greater agony than bearing an untold story inside you.'

Maya Angelou, memoirist, poet and civil rights activist

Publishing avenues

Choosing which path you want to go down when it comes to publishing your hard work is one of the biggest decisions you will make as an author. The history of publishing is fascinating, beginning in 1439, when Johannes Gutenberg became the first European to use movable type and set up what became known as a printing press.[7] Because Gutenberg's design was large, heavy and expensive, this remained the sole way books could be printed for five whole centuries.

It wasn't until 1979 that the first huge barrier to being a published author was removed with the introduction of desktop publishing. It was then that self-publishing became a trend, and many who were still dedicated to the traditional form of engaging a publisher to print and distribute their books coined the term 'vanity publishing' in disdain. In their eyes, those who could not get the attention or investment of a traditional publishing house were simply taking matters into their own hands to satisfy their own egos. Thank goodness times have changed!

The early days of self-publishing meant aspiring authors would print runs on consignment, sell by mail-order and drive around to bookshops with the hope of moving their carloads of books and making a name for themselves.

The arrival of print on demand, as digital printing processes became more advanced, made it economically viable to print single copies or small batches to order. Digital publishing lacked a payment mechanism until 1998, when pioneering publishers and authors began to sell books online.

Publishing avenues

Sony released the first ebook reader in 2004, followed by the Kindle eReader from Amazon in 2007, which came with a vast retail store attached. From that moment, everything changed for authors. Agents, publishers and wholesalers were no longer vital to the publishing process and aspiring authors had more choice and control over their work. In many cases, only an online distributor-retailer stood between writer and reader.

There has been a constant upward trend of people self-publishing since 2012, and it has become a widely accepted way to share your work with the world. Being an 'indie' author means owning a successful writing and publishing business that is not dependent on *any* single outlet, but instead being truly independent and in control of every decision.

While self-publishing is no longer tarred with the blanket 'vanity' label, any modern reference to 'vanity' publishing is to describe publishers who invest very little, if any, resources in refining work they take on, largely publishing manuscripts as is.

On my podcast, Kym Cousins, the author of *Selling With Heart*, shared her thoughts about publishing her book.

> 'There are two things you can invest in it: time and money. If you need to invest the money in the process, then be fairly clear about how you're going to get a return on that investment. Now, for some people, their return on investment is not necessarily that you're going to sell thousands of books; that return on investment could be that the book leads to a lot of other things. It's a tool to be able to spread the word. It's a tool to help you in your business in the offering that you

have. Or it could be for some people, it's simply a cathartic thing to get something off their chest.'

You can watch the full interview here:

Having a traditional publishing contract might be your dream goal, or you might place more value in maintaining control and reaping the rewards of book sales directly. But as you will come to learn as you move through this section, there are pros and cons to every publishing avenue.

> There is no right or wrong, but knowing what is important to you will help guide your decision on which path you take to transform your manuscript from an electronic document into a tangible book.

We are going to take a look at the three most common publishing pathways so you can begin to choose your own adventure. These are:

1. Traditional/trade
2. Self

Publishing avenues

3. Independent
   - Vanity
   - Hybrid
   - Publishing service providers

To help you decide what each path looks like, I will guide you through what is covered in each and then list the pros and cons, so you have everything you need to make an informed choice about your publishing journey.

Traditional/trade

For many aspiring authors, traditional publishing represents the ultimate dream. There's a certain magic attached to being able to say, 'My book was published by Penguin,' or 'I'm with Allen & Unwin'. It's a badge of honour, a mark of legitimacy. After all, these are the publishers who've been shaping bookshelves for generations.

But while traditional publishing is often held up as the gold standard, it's important to look beyond the prestige and understand what's really involved because the journey is layered, competitive, and at times, confronting.

A traditional publisher, also known as a trade publisher, takes full responsibility for producing, distributing and selling your book. If they accept your manuscript, they buy the rights to publish it and then cover the cost of editing, designing, printing and distributing your work. For many authors, the most immediate benefit is the advance payment. This is an upfront sum paid to you when a publishing house acquires your manuscript. Beyond that, there's relief in knowing that you're not out of pocket for any of the production or packaging. Your job is to write the book; theirs is to polish it, print it and place it in readers' hands.

One of the strongest advantages of this pathway is the built-in infrastructure. Traditional publishers have teams of professionals behind every project, including editors who know how to shape a manuscript into something commercially viable, designers who understand market trends, publicists who speak the language of the media, and most importantly, deep and longstanding relationships with bookstores and distributors. That kind of reach is hard to replicate when you're publishing independently.

However, with everything in life, there are pros and cons. When you sign with a traditional publisher, you also sign over creative control. You may have strong opinions about your title or your cover, but ultimately, those decisions lie with the publisher. They may alter your manuscript in ways you hadn't anticipated or delay its release for strategic reasons, sometimes for months or even years. This might feel personal, but it's not. Publishing is a business, and publishers have to make decisions based on timing, trends and launching at the best time to maximise opportunity for return on investment.

> It's also worth noting that once you've handed over the rights to your work, the publisher owns the book.

Publishing avenues

That includes deciding how it's marketed, what territories it's sold in, and whether and when international editions or audiobooks are created. Many first-time authors are surprised by just how much control they relinquish. The deal can be worth it, of course, but only if you go in with eyes wide open.

Another surprise for many is just how low the royalty rates can be. While that advance can feel like a windfall, royalties, which are the earnings you make from each sale, are often modest. For debut authors, it's not uncommon to earn around one dollar per book sold. That can improve as your profile grows, but it's far from a guarantee.

There's also the marketing myth to contend with. Many authors believe that once they sign a traditional deal, the publisher will take care of everything, including building their audience and landing media coverage. While publishers do have marketing teams and budgets, those resources are allocated strategically. High-profile authors and books with mass commercial appeal will receive more attention, while others may receive a more modest push. Some authors land national tours and television spots, while others receive a press release template and a polite suggestion to start building their social media following.

Smaller publishers can sometimes offer a more personal touch. They might not have the massive distribution networks of the big players, but they're often more collaborative and better aligned with niche markets. For certain genres or topic areas, a passionate boutique publisher can be a better fit than a big-name brand.

The challenge, of course, is getting in the door. The competition is fierce. Some publishers still accept unsolicited manuscripts, but many don't, which means you'll need to go through a literary agent. Agents can help you shape your manuscript, craft a compelling pitch and knock on the right doors, but they typically take a commission (usually around fifteen per cent), and their time is also in high demand.

Whether you're submitting directly or via an agent, one thing is guaranteed: you're competing against hundreds, sometimes thousands, of other writers.

This doesn't mean the traditional path is impossible. It just means it requires patience, persistence and a clear understanding of what you want from the experience. If you're pursuing traditional publishing purely for the prestige, it's worth asking whether that alone is enough. But if your goal is broad reach, global distribution and the backing of a well-established team, this could absolutely be the right path.

Ultimately, the best thing you can do is research. Look closely at different publishers and what they offer. Some are strong on distribution, but light on publicity. Others invest heavily in promotion but may lack the power to get you onto bookshelves in stores. Align yourself with a publisher who shares your values, understands your genre and is enthusiastic about your message.

I always say you've got nothing to lose by dipping your toe in the water to see if the interest is there. If you are fortunate enough to get a response, don't get swept away in the romanticism of being 'chosen'. Whatever you do, read the contract. Every. Word.

Publishing avenues

Of. It. Get a second opinion if you need to. Once you sign, you're in a business relationship. It should serve both your dreams and your best interests.

Tips for submitting your manuscript to traditional publishers or literary agents

If you've decided traditional publishing could be for you, there is one crucial hurdle: the submission process. Submitting your book to a traditional publisher is as much about strategy and professionalism as it is about storytelling. The quality of your manuscript matters deeply, but so does how you present it.

Publishers receive countless submissions every month, and depending on their workload and available time, some are skimmed, some are read in full and some are dismissed almost immediately due to common, avoidable mistakes.

Your goal is to stand out for the *right* reasons, so here are some practical tips to help you submit your manuscript in a way that gives it the best possible chance of making it past the slush pile and into the hands of a decision-maker.

 Research

Not every publisher accepts unsolicited submissions and not every publisher or agent is right for your book. Take the time to research who publishes books in your genre, what their submission guidelines are and whether they're currently open to new authors. Visit their website, read their recent titles and make sure your work aligns with their list.

Follow submission guidelines

This might sound obvious, but you'd be surprised how many authors get this wrong. Publishers and literary agents receive more submissions each month than you probably want to know. If they ask for the first three chapters and a synopsis, don't send your whole manuscript. If they want double spacing and twelve-point Times New Roman, don't get fancy. Submitting exactly what they ask for shows professionalism and respect for their process.

 Polish your manuscript

Traditional publishers don't expect perfection, but they do expect a manuscript that's been proofread and thoughtfully crafted. You would never send through your shitty first draft, but a second draft that has been refined and restructured from your initial brain dump will pass. First impressions matter.

 Craft a compelling cover letter

This is your first chance to pitch your book (and yourself). Be concise, professional and enthusiastic. Most publishers will provide guidelines for what they need from you, but if you've found a rare one that doesn't have this readily available to you, include:

- a short introduction
- a one-paragraph hook or blurb for your book
- why you're submitting to this publisher

Publishing avenues

- any relevant writing credentials or personal connection to the subject
- proof of a social media following or email list.

Think of it like a job application. You're not just selling a story, you're showing them you're someone they'd want to work with.

 Include a strong synopsis

I understand how incredibly hard it is to condense your book into one or two pages. But a synopsis is essential. It should clearly outline the plot and focus on clarity, not cliffhangers. They're not reading it to be surprised; they're reading it to assess structure and substance.

 Be patient

Response times can be long, anywhere from three to six months, occasionally longer. While you're waiting, keep writing, refining your pitch, or submitting to other publishers (if their guidelines allow simultaneous submissions). Always note in your letter if you are submitting to multiple places.

 Keep track

Create a spreadsheet or document to record where you've submitted, the date, what materials you sent and any responses received. This will help you stay organised and avoid double submissions.

Ignite & Write: The Published Author

To save time, head to *The Structured Author* resources and download a ready-made Publishing Submission template you can fill in:

 Don't give up

Many bestselling authors were rejected dozens of times before landing a deal. Keep refining, keep writing and keep submitting. The right publisher for your book is out there. Your job is to keep knocking on doors until it opens.

Rejection

Rejections are part of the process. Often they are about genre/brand fit, timing or market trends. Resist the urge to reply defensively or emotionally because it's rarely personal. If you're lucky enough to receive feedback from the publisher or literary agent, take it as a gift. Learn from it and grow.

Because approaching a traditional publisher is about trying to capture their attention, even something as simple as a flat cover letter could be the minor thing that lands your manuscript on the reject pile.

Please do not be discouraged if you receive a rejection letter or no letter at all, for that matter. Do not see it as a failure, or worse,

Publishing avenues

that no one thinks there is any value in what you have created. Instead, realise that perhaps you simply haven't found the right publisher for you.

Some of the world's biggest-selling authors were initially sent packing:

- Stephen King's first big novel, *Carrie*, was rejected thirty times. He tossed it in the wastebasket, but his wife fished it out. It was published in 1975 and he had earned $39 million from it by 2012.[8]
- J.K. Rowling, the first author billionaire, had *Harry Potter and the Philosopher's Stone* rejected by a dozen British publishing houses and reportedly got into print, for a £1500 advance, only after the eight-year-old daughter of a publisher pleaded for it.[9]
- *Chicken Soup for the Soul*, the iconic series of inspirational books, received one hundred and forty-four rejections before becoming a bestseller.[10]
- *Zen and the Art of Motorcycle Maintenance*, a philosophical work by Robert Pirsig, received one hundred and twenty-one rejections before being accepted for publication in 1974 and going on to sell millions of copies. It remains a literary icon.[11]
- Lisa Genova wrote *Still Alice*, and after getting little positive feedback and no takers from the query process, she opted to self-publish her book. Eventually, it was acquired and reissued by Gallery Books, an imprint of Simon & Schuster. It proceeded

to spend forty weeks on *The New York Times Best Sellers* list. In 2015, Julianne Moore won an Academy Award for portraying the eponymous Alice.[12]

Lisa's case is a perfect example of how you never shut the door to potential publishers, even if you do initially choose to go with another possible publishing avenue.

As evident from each instance, there was one character trait that got these authors over the line – persistence.

IN THE KNOW: PROS AND CONS OF TRADITIONAL PUBLISHING

Pros

- The publisher takes on the cost of producing your book.
- You may receive an advance for your work.
- The publisher may have their own distribution network set up. This may allow them to get your book into brick-and-mortar shops and large department stores.
- You may receive marketing assistance.
- A relationship with a publisher will allow you easier access to pitch future books.

Cons

- You sign over the rights to your book.
- You may have some input into the editing, styling and production of your book, but the publisher ultimately has the final say because your work is their investment.
- Your book release will be determined by the publisher. This could mean an immediate release, or that it sits in a pipeline for several months, even a couple of years, until they feel the market is 'right'.
- 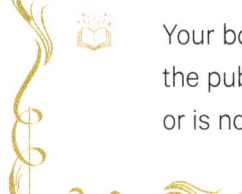 Your book may be taken out of circulation once the publisher deems it has fulfilled its purpose or is no longer worth reprinting.

Self-publishing

There's something incredibly liberating about self-publishing. For years, it carried a stigma, dismissed as vanity publishing or seen as a last resort for authors who 'couldn't get a deal'. Thankfully, that outdated view has been firmly left in the past. These days, self-publishing is not only respected, it's often celebrated as a powerful and strategic move, especially for authors who want control, speed and ownership of their work.

So what does it actually mean to self-publish? At its core, self-publishing means you are the publisher. That means you're in charge of every decision, and you can do it all yourself if you have the time and skills.

That can feel overwhelming at first. It's not unusual to find yourself wondering about how to format a book or write a blurb. The good news? There are countless resources out there to help you, from free YouTube tutorials and industry blogs to online courses and author support communities.

Hint: You can check out my YouTube channel for some helpful writing and publishing tips:

When you don't want to DIY something, you can outsource it through publishing support services, which you will learn more about very soon. In fact, many successful self-published authors choose to focus on their strengths, like writing and vision, and hire help for the rest.

One of the biggest advantages of self-publishing is full creative and financial control.

There's no one telling you to wait eighteen months for market timing or insisting you cut a chapter that doesn't 'fit the brand'. If you finish your manuscript and want it to be live within a few weeks, that's entirely possible; you're the boss.

Publishing avenues

The return on investment is another major drawcard of self-publishing. With traditional publishing, your royalties can be as low as five per cent of the book's retail price. But when you self-publish, the profit margins are significantly higher. Let's break it down. If you sell a book for $24.99 through a traditional publisher, you might walk away with $1 per sale. If you self-publish and sell that same book, you could be earning closer to $15 per copy. That adds up quickly, especially if you've built an engaged audience or have a plan for ongoing sales.

Of course, higher rewards come with higher responsibilities. One of the biggest realities of self-publishing is that you fund the production of your book upfront. You'll need to budget for editing, cover design, interior formatting, ISBNs and possibly software or platform subscriptions. This is an investment, but it's also one you have full control over. You can scale up or down depending on your needs and goals and whatever you can execute yourself will save you the fees to pay a publishing support service to do it.

The other reality is marketing. There's no in-house publicist or bookstore sales rep. You are your own marketing department. For some authors, this is a dream come true because they love the strategy, the visibility and the entrepreneurial hustle. For others, it can feel daunting. But again, there's flexibility. You can do it all yourself, learn as you go, or hire help. The key is understanding that the success of your book is directly tied to how well it's positioned, promoted and maintained in the market over time.

Unfortunately, many self-published authors can be tripped up by a lack of knowledge. After all, you don't know what you don't know! There are a lot of finer points, especially on the design and technical side of things, that can catch first-timers unawares. Luckily, there are thriving online groups, author forums and mentorship programs filled with generous writers who share what they've learned.

There are platforms like Amazon KDP, IngramSpark, Draft2Digital and others that provide most of the information you need to DIY and handle distribution while giving you full control over your book's file and metadata. Self-publishing does take a lot more time to learn all the moving parts, but for many authors, the creative and financial payoff is more than worth it.

IN THE KNOW: PROS AND CONS OF SELF-PUBLISHING

Pros

- You make all the decisions from the title, cover, structure and pricing to the release date.
- You retain one hundred per cent of your intellectual property and publishing rights.
- You can publish your book as soon as it's ready, no twelve to eighteen-month industry delays.
- You keep the majority of your profits (often sixty to one hundred per cent),

Publishing avenues

- depending on your publishing platform and distribution choices.
- You choose how to promote your book and when.
- Publishing under your own name or imprint helps establish authority, especially for entrepreneurs, coaches and thought leaders.
- Platforms like Amazon KDP and IngramSpark make it easy to get your book into online retailers and even bookstores, libraries and schools.
- Your self-published book can become the foundation for courses, speaking gigs, coaching programs and more.

Cons

- There are many skills you have to learn in order to successfully self-publish.
- You may need to budget for help with areas you cannot DIY.
- Managing all the moving parts takes time and energy.
- If you're doing it yourself, you'll need to learn the ropes of publishing, distribution, metadata and marketing.
- Without a publisher's stamp of approval, some readers or retailers may (unfairly) view self-

- published books as less professional (note: it's not!).
- Promotion, visibility, media outreach and sales are on your shoulders, unless you outsource or build a team.
- A professionally produced self-published book is indistinguishable from a traditionally published one, but if corners are cut, it can show.

Independent

The path to publishing is no longer a two-lane highway of traditional versus self-publishing; it's now a multi-lane highway, filled with independent options that promise varying levels of support, partnership and investment.

Independent publishing can be an empowering middle ground for authors who want more control than traditional publishing offers, but more support than self-publishing typically provides. However, not all independent publishers are created equal. Understanding the differences could save you time, money and heartache.

Independent publishing – or indie publishing – is hands-down my favourite model, and it's also where the majority of my clients tend to land. It really is the best of both worlds.

Publishing avenues

With an indie publisher, you retain full control and ownership of your manuscript and your rights, but you also have a team of publishing professionals behind you. That means you're not alone in trying to find the right editor, graphic designer, typesetter, or distributor – they're already part of the team and they're all working toward your book's success.

The indie publishing model is structured and professional. There's a defined process, a clear workflow, and the end result is a book that meets the standards of the trade. Most importantly – it's your book. You call the shots on cover design, title, tone, timeline and pricing. The publisher is there to guide and support, not override.

This model can require some upfront investment, yes – but you're investing in quality and you still reap the rewards. You're not giving away rights or waiting around for gatekeepers. Indie publishers often have established distribution networks too, so your book can reach online stores, libraries, audiobook platforms and independent bookshops without you having to figure that out alone.

In my author interview series *Ignite & Write Podcast*, I've spoken to authors from all walks of life, including a few high-profile international bestsellers. These are people who've experienced all three publishing streams – traditional, self and indie. Every single one of them, without hesitation, said they preferred the indie model. That speaks volumes.

> And here's another beautiful thing to keep in mind: choosing indie publishing does not lock you out of traditional publishing down the track.

In fact, I've seen several authors self- or independently publish incredible books, go on to sell thousands of copies, win awards, build loyal audiences – and suddenly, traditional publishers who once turned them away come knocking. The power dynamic flips. You're no longer chasing them. They're chasing you.

I have chosen to focus on the three main types of independent publishers – vanity, hybrid and publishing service providers – so that by the end of this section, you'll have a clear understanding of what each model offers, how to tell the difference between a genuine publishing partner and a predatory one, and most importantly, what type of publishing relationship is best suited to your goals as an author.

This isn't about saying which is the 'right' path for everyone. It's about equipping you with all the information so you can make an educated choice about the right path for you.

Vanity publisher

While its moniker was once designated by publishing purists to reflect anyone who used a non-traditional publishing route, vanity publishing now has a much more specific definition; it is businesses who will charge authors to publish their work

Publishing avenues

with very little professional input to get an author's work up to industry standards. While vanity publishers may appear to offer a convenient path to getting your book published (after all, they will take on anything and everything), the truth is they often overpromise, underdeliver and charge a premium for minimal return.

For most serious authors, the cons far outweigh the pros, especially when there are more empowering, transparent and ethical publishing alternatives available.

One of my biggest peeves is seeing authors pour their heart and soul into their manuscript only to be taken advantage of by cowboys in the publishing industry. Not only does it suck the passion out of your original vision, but it can leave you thousands of dollars in the red and no longer in control of your own intellectual property (IP).

So how do you avoid it?

- Be wary of publishers who reach out to you with a publishing offer. These are very likely scammers who are prepared to take you to the bank over your desire to be published.
- Check the email address of any offers in your inbox. If it is a generic Gmail address with no business name, no website, no phone number, no link to their social media, consider it likely to be fake.
- If you are considering a lesser-known publisher, conduct an internet search with the business name plus 'scam' and see what comes up. You can also try

the business name plus 'reviews' and make sure the reviews you are reading are from a third-party website and not the carefully curated ones they have selected to put up on their own website.

 There is also a great resource you can tap into that flags dodgy publishers. Visit: writerbeware.blog

 Examine communications carefully. Here's an example of what you commonly might find in a letter from a vanity publisher:

RE: We'd Love to Publish [Manuscript Title] With You!

Dear [author name],

First of all – congratulations! We are so thrilled you've entrusted us with your manuscript. It's not every day that we come across a voice as unique and promising as yours, and we genuinely believe your book deserves to be out in the world.

After reviewing [manuscript title], our editorial team was unanimous: this is a story that needs to be told. We see real potential here – not just as a book, but as something that could truly inspire readers and change lives.

Unfortunately, we do not have any positions open within our traditional publishing suite, however, we're confident that with the right support, your book can reach its audience.

At [business name], we believe that every author is special, and we take great pride in offering a warm, collaborative process from start to finish. That's why we're offering you a place in our Author

Publishing avenues

Partnership Program – a tailored package designed to elevate your manuscript to professional standards and get it into the hands of readers worldwide.

Your publishing experience will include:

- dedicated editing and design support
- a personalised cover to reflect your story
- ISBN assignment and registration
- print and ebook distribution through major global channels
- a custom marketing starter kit
- ongoing author support from our friendly publishing advisors.

To ensure we can give your book the care and attention it deserves, we ask for a one-time contribution of just [$X thousand] to help cover production and setup costs. Rest assured, all royalties from your book sales (a generous ten per cent) go directly to you – we only succeed when you do.

If you'd like to move forward, simply review the enclosed agreement and return it by [deadline], along with the initial deposit of [$X hundred] to secure your place in our program.

We truly believe in your work, and we can't wait to welcome you into the [business name] family.

With heartfelt excitement,
[publisher contact name]

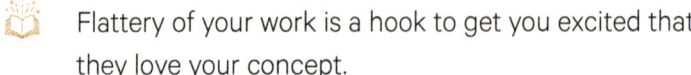

Here are the red flags with a letter like this:

- Flattery of your work is a hook to get you excited that they love your concept.

- Most vanity publishers accept almost every submission, regardless of quality. Phrases like 'careful evaluation' create the illusion of selectivity to flatter authors and boost credibility.

- A common trait of vanity publishers is that they claim to have a trade publishing option, but there is no current availability. They can then play up how they believe in your work and how their package is the next best option to get your book published.

- Their praise is generic and rarely backed by actual market plans or data. It's a tactic to emotionally hook authors. There is often no personalisation or understanding of your book and its content, although some companies are using AI to fill in the blanks. So if any mention of your work sounds suspiciously like what you've already circulated on your website or on social media, they've likely sourced it from there.

- Bundling basic services (editing, cover design, ISBN, distribution) and selling them as a package is common with vanity presses. These services are often overpriced and of variable quality.

- Calling the fee a 'one-time contribution' instead of a payment or charge is a classic euphemism.

Publishing avenues

- Phrases like 'we only succeed when you do' hide the reality that their revenue comes from your payment, not book sales.
- Referring to authors as part of a 'family' or 'partnership program' makes it harder to say no.
- A request for money up front is the hallmark of a vanity press. *You pay them*, rather than the other way around. They profit from authors, not readers.
- Some vanity publishers offer 'high royalties' to make the deal sound generous. But if few or no books are sold – due to poor marketing or distribution – it's meaningless.
- The deadline adds pressure to act quickly, limiting your time to research or seek professional advice.

One rule of thumb I would like you to anchor right away is that there are two clear paths for aspiring authors:

1. You are paid for your work with an advance and/or royalties and do not pay for production.
2. You pay for production and therefore do not share royalties for your work.

I have seen far too many people being approached by these dodgy operators who promise the world, then ask for the author to chip in for production costs, retain ownership of your work and also have the audacity to acquire the vast majority of sales royalties as well.

In other cases, they request the author pay upfront for production costs, and then the publisher will take the royalties until the 'cost of production' is paid off. Only then, the author will receive royalties. What most authors do not realise is that these businesses are essentially being paid by you twice, and because they have made their money, they will not be actively marketing your book so that *you* can make money. Furthermore, how would you know how many sales you have made anyway? They will have all that data, so they can (and do) fabricate figures to make it appear that you have not reached your quota.

Please avoid these operations because you are being cheated out of your hard-earned money.

Any trade publisher worth their salt will not require you to pay for the creation of your book. They will see value in what you have written and be willing to back you as an investment and help to make your book a success.

Similarly, any reputable hybrid publisher or publishing support service will charge you for the services they provide to create your book and not enforce a contract that allows them to stand in the background with their hand out, expecting royalties once you become successful.

As the old adage goes, if something is too good to be true, it probably is. So protect yourself and do your due diligence to select the best partner for your publishing journey.

Publishing avenues

IN THE KNOW: PROS AND CONS OF USING A VANITY PUBLISHER

Pros

- You can often have a book published quickly, with minimal gatekeeping.
- No rejection. They accept almost any manuscript, so your work won't be subject to rigorous editorial selection.
- Most offer editing, design and printing in one place, which may feel convenient for first-time authors.
- Your book will appear professionally published at first glance, which may appeal to some.
- If you're looking to publish without having to manage the process or learn the industry, vanity publishers often take over completely.

Cons

- Vanity publishers make their money from you, not from selling books to readers. This is the biggest red flag in the industry.
- Editing, design and layout are often outsourced or templated, resulting in subpar books that damage your credibility.

- Promises of global reach rarely deliver. Your book may be listed online, but not actively marketed or stocked anywhere meaningful.
- Rights and royalties are often unclear or unfair. You may pay thousands and still have limited control over your own book.
- Industry professionals (including booksellers, reviewers and agents) often see vanity-published books as amateurish or low-quality.
- Despite the claim of a one-off fee, many authors find themselves upsold on additional services like marketing, editing, or even buying back their own books.
- Unlike traditional or legitimate hybrid publishers, vanity presses have no financial stake in how your book performs in the market.
- Despite large upfront costs, many authors sell fewer than one hundred copies, often to family and friends only.

Hybrid publisher

Hybrid publishing lives at the intersection between self-publishing and trade publishing. In a hybrid model, you contribute financially to the production of your book, and in return, you gain access to a publisher's professional team,

Publishing avenues

processes and resources. The hybrid publisher handles editing, design, printing and often even distribution.

The thing that makes hybrids different from vanities is that a legitimate model will not require you to sign over the rights to your work. This means you are officially the copyright owner of your work and have the final decision over every part of the process.

If you are tapping into the publisher's distribution network, you may be required to share a slice of sales royalties to compensate them for pushing your book out, but you will equally have the choice whether to engage with that or stick with managing your own platform, such as Ingram Spark or Amazon KDP, which you will learn more about later in this book in the Product platforms chapter. Either way, you will still earn higher royalties than you would through a trade-published book.

> Hybrid publishers operate as businesses that earn their revenue from author contributions, not from book sales.

This means you'll likely be asked to pay upfront or on a milestone basis, depending on the package and provider. The benefit? You still own your rights. You still get a say in how your book looks and feels. And you benefit from working with a team that knows what they're doing. If you have done your homework, you will find businesses that have teams of people who've produced dozens, if not hundreds, of books and know exactly what will make yours stand out in a competitive market.

The downside? Not all hybrid publishers are created equal. Some offer genuine quality and care, while others can feel more like glorified vanity presses. Always do your due diligence. Ask to see previous work. Talk to other authors. Most importantly, make sure the contract terms support *you* as the author, not just the publisher's bottom line.

IN THE KNOW: PROS AND CONS OF USING A HYBRID PUBLISHER

Pros

- Shared investment between author and publisher.
- Professional editing, design and production included.
- More creative control than traditional publishing.
- Faster publishing timelines.
- Retain more rights and higher royalty rates.
- Support with distribution and marketing (varies by provider).
- Often more transparent and collaborative than vanity publishers.

Publishing avenues

Cons

- You pay upfront or at project milestones.
- Quality and integrity vary widely across providers.
- Some hybrids blur the line with vanity publishing.
- Not always selective – some accept nearly every manuscript.
- Marketing support may be limited or generic.
- Less prestige and recognition than traditional publishing.
- You may be tied to set packages and unable to choose what you need.
- Sales success is still largely up to you.

Publishing service providers

As you explore the world of independent publishing, you'll soon discover there's a third path that offers professional support without taking over control. This option is often referred to as author support services or publishing service providers. They're not publishers in the traditional sense, but rather a team you can hire to help bring your book to life.

The key difference here is that you remain the publisher. You're in charge of the decisions, the creative direction, the distribution and the outcomes. You don't hand over your rights or royalties. You don't give away control. Essentially, you are self-publishing but with an additional step – you bring in experts to handle the parts of the process you'd prefer not to navigate alone.

> In many ways, accessing publishing support services is the most empowering option on the publishing spectrum.

You're not waiting for permission. You're not subject to publishing trends or gatekeeper decisions. You get to create and share your work exactly how and when you want to. For first-time authors and seasoned professionals alike, it's become a legitimate publishing pathway that produces professional results.

This can be incredibly empowering, especially for authors who are clear on their vision but want to ensure their book meets professional standards. You can choose exactly what support you need, whether that's editing, cover design, layout or even help with your publishing admin, like ISBN registration and distribution platform setup. It's a flexible, collaborative model where you're building your own publishing path, but with trusted professionals at your side.

In case you were wondering, this is where the Ignite & Write Publishing wheelhouse sits.

Publishing avenues

Unlike vanity publishers, publishing service providers are transparent about what they offer and how much it costs. You're not being sold a dream or lured in with vague promises of bestseller status.

You're hiring a team to do a job, and when done well, the result is a book that looks, reads and functions just like something produced by a traditional press. The only difference? It's entirely yours. Your name. Your imprint. Your royalties. Your rules.

Of course, with that ownership comes responsibility. You'll still need to steer the ship when it comes to marketing and promotion, and you'll need to stay engaged in the process by approving designs, reviewing edits, setting your pricing and making the final calls. But for many authors, that's exactly what they want. They're not looking to hand their book over; they're looking to build something that feels aligned, authentic and entirely their own.

Engaging publishing support services is a powerful choice for those who value both independence and professionalism. It's self-publishing, but not solo publishing. When done with care and clarity, it's one of the most rewarding ways to bring your book into the world.

IN THE KNOW: PROS AND CONS OF PUBLISHING SERVICE PROVIDERS

Pros

- You keep all rights to your book.
- You have final say over any decisions related to editing, styling and production of your book.
- You have the support of a professional team that knows what they are doing and can provide expert guidance.
- Flexible support, as you can choose only the services you need.
- More affordable than hybrid publishing teams when used strategically.
- Faster turnaround times.
- You can release the book whenever you choose. This allows you to either go for immediate release or hold onto it to release at a time more beneficial for leveraging. We will go into this more in the marketing chapters of this book.
- Because you own the rights to your book, it will stay in circulation for as long as you want it to be.
- You can build your own imprint or publishing brand.

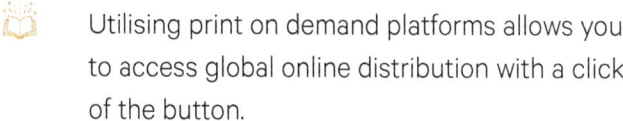

Publishing avenues

- Utilising print on demand platforms allows you to access global online distribution with a click of the button.
- If being an Amazon bestseller is on your agenda, you can implement processes to boost your chances of getting that coveted badge.
- Ideal for entrepreneurial authors who want control without doing it all alone.

Cons

- Requires investment of both time and money for the support services to produce your book.
- May not have built-in marketing or sales support.
- Need to complete due diligence to gauge the quality of the work being produced by the service and ensure the team is qualified and professional, not hobbyists.
- Less prestige and recognition than traditional publishing.
- Sales success is still largely up to you.

There's no one-size-fits-all approach. Each of these models offers different degrees of control, investment, support and reward. The question isn't which one is *best*, but rather which one aligns with your vision, your goals, your timeline and your budget.

Whether you want full creative freedom with expert support, or a collaborative partner who helps you shoulder the publishing load, there's an option that fits. The key is to stay informed, ask questions and never settle for a publishing experience that doesn't respect your voice, your work or your worth.

Publishing avenues

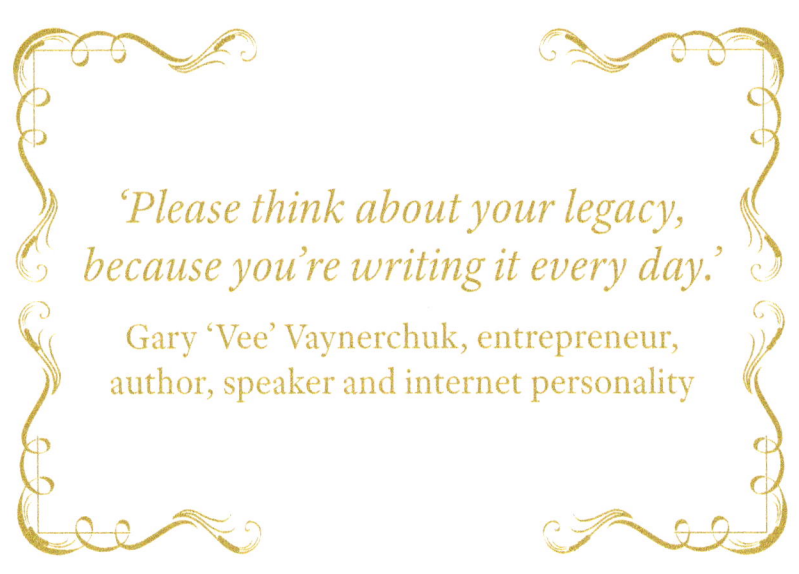

'Please think about your legacy, because you're writing it every day.'

Gary 'Vee' Vaynerchuk, entrepreneur, author, speaker and internet personality

'Excellence is never an accident. It is always the result of high intention, sincere effort and intelligent execution; it represents the wise choice of many alternatives – choice, not chance, determines your destiny.'

Aristotle, ancient Greek philosopher

Product platforms

Once your book is published, the next major decision for you to make is how you are going to deliver it to your audience. If you have gone down the trade route, this will be taken care of for you. But if you are in the indie or self-publishing camps, this is your next big consideration.

The ball really is in your court, and as you know, you have the power to choose your own adventure because authors have more options than ever before. You can print physical copies in bulk using offset printing or take advantage of the flexibility of print on demand. You might choose to release an ebook, ready to download at the tap of a screen, or record an audiobook that allows your voice to bring your words to life.

Once you've decided on the format, distribution becomes the bridge between you and your readers, whether that's through online platforms, bookstores, libraries or even direct sales. Each of these avenues comes with its own benefits and challenges. Some are cost-effective but offer limited reach. Others have broad visibility but tighter margins. Some give you complete control, while others require you to work within established systems.

I'll walk you through each option, helping you weigh the possibilities and build a publishing plan that works for your unique situation. Whether you dream of seeing your book on bookstore shelves, in people's earbuds, or simply reaching readers wherever they are, there is a path forward.

Product platforms

The great thing about this part of the process is that you are not locked into one method forever. Many authors start with one and then expand, or use a combination to best reach their ideal reader.

Offset printing

Offset printing is the traditional route, the one used by big-name publishers for decades. Technically speaking, it is a process where your book's pages are transferred (or 'offset') from a plate to a rubber blanket, and then onto the paper. It's ideal for printing hundreds or thousands of copies at once, and it's how most traditionally published books are produced.

If you're planning to sell a significant number of books or already have strong interest from readers, this method can make a lot of sense.

One of the biggest advantages of offset printing is that the more copies you print, the cheaper each copy becomes. This is known as the cost per unit (CPU). So if you're confident in your sales potential, a larger print run of say, five thousand copies could bring your per-book cost down significantly compared to a smaller run of five hundred. To use *The Structured Author* as a real-life example, a single copy is $11.34, the CPU for five hundred copies is $10.21 and the CPU for five thousand copies is $7.94. If you choose to print offshore, you can potentially get the CPU down to a few dollars a book, but be prepared to wait extra time for the books to be shipped and clear customs before they can get to your door.

This became a real headache for authors during the covid-19 pandemic, when the docks were backed up with containers upon containers because there were no customs officers to inspect the shipments. Some authors were forced to launch without a book in hand, which is not ideal. It sucks a bit of the air out of the excitement of the event, right? So if your publisher is using an offshore printer, be sure to add in a few extra weeks as a buffer to allow for those unexpected delays. After all, it's better to have them early than to be scrambling at the last minute.

Offset also gives you more control over the physical feel of your book.

You can choose from a wider range of finishes, paper stock, trim sizes and binding options – even gold foil stamping if that's your thing! If you're dreaming of a hardcover edition, a coffee-table-style book, or a premium print experience, offset is often the way to go for the best quality.

But, and this is an important but, you need to be realistic. Offset printing requires a significant upfront investment, both in cost and in logistics. Once those books are printed, they're yours to store, manage and sell. You don't want to end up with boxes of unsold books taking up space in your garage (yes, it happens more than you think).

If you're considering offset printing but unsure how many books you'll actually move, pre-sales can be a great way to test the waters. They help you measure real interest before you commit

Product platforms

to a print run, reducing your financial risk and giving you the confidence to move forward with eyes wide open.

Offset printing can absolutely work for self-published authors, but I recommend that you back it up with a plan. If you've got an audience, strong pre-orders, or clear distribution channels, it can be a smart, cost-effective choice. Just make sure your vision matches the reality of what you can confidently deliver.

IN THE KNOW: PROS AND CONS FOR OFFSET PRINTING

Pros

- Much lower per-copy cost at scale.
- Superior print quality and finish options (hardcovers, matte/gloss covers, foiling, embossing, etc).
- More control over materials, binding and customisation.
- Ideal for large launches, events and bulk distribution.
- Stronger perception of professionalism in retail channels.
- Ability to have selected pages printed in colour or gloss pages.

Cons

- High upfront costs (often thousands of dollars).
- Requires accurate sales forecasting – risk of over-ordering.
- Storage, fulfilment and shipping are the author's responsibility.
- Longer lead times (four to twelve weeks or more).
- Revisions are costly once books are printed.

Print on demand

Print on demand, or POD as it's often called, has completely transformed the way authors can publish and share their books with the world. As the name suggests, this model means your book is only printed when someone places an order. There's no bulk printing in advance, no guesswork about how many copies to produce and no towering stack of unsold books taking up space in your garage. This low-risk, flexible model is an absolute game-changer and my favourite way for my authors to get their work out into the world.

The beauty of POD is its simplicity. You upload your files (or your publishing service provider will do this for you), choose your specs and fill in the metadata, and once your book is live, every time someone clicks 'buy,' a single copy is printed and shipped automatically.

Product platforms

There are no upfront print costs because you're only paying for books once they've been sold. That alone takes a huge weight off your shoulders, especially when you're launching into the publishing world for the first time. There's also no need to organise storage or manage complicated logistics. Services like Amazon KDP and IngramSpark handle all of that behind the scenes.

IngramSpark, in particular, has become a major player in this space. As part of the Ingram Content Group, they give authors access to an enormous global network of over forty-five thousand retailers, libraries and online platforms across the world. This means your book isn't just available to order from one place, it can potentially be ordered from anywhere books are sold. For those of us who want to reach readers beyond our local networks or social media circles, that kind of distribution power is gold.

> It is a real thrill that once we let our authors know their book is going live, they can conduct online searches and see where their book is showing up.

It goes to the top dogs like Amazon, Barnes & Noble, Booktopia, Waterstones, Walmart, Book Depository, Books-A-Million and Target. It's incredibly exciting. Then you might see your book on the shelf of an indie bookstore or in the library, because they can all order from that service too.

That said, print on demand does come with a few trade-offs. Because books are printed one at a time, the per-copy cost is higher than it would be if you ordered in bulk via offset printing. While the quality is great, you are unable to have more of the fancier things, such as glossy photo pages in the centre of the book, or special touches like foiling and embossing. If you have a highly visual or premium format in mind, like a coffee table book or a gift edition, you might find these limitations a little restrictive and will have to go for offset.

When publishing through POD platforms, authors need to account for the retailer discount, which typically ranges from forty to fifty-five per cent off the book's retail price. This discount is what online and physical retailers take as their share for selling your book. It means if you set your book's recommended retail price (RRP) at $30 and you offer a fifty per cent discount, the retailer keeps $15 before any printing costs are deducted. It's a crucial factor to consider when setting your price because if you don't build in that margin, you could end up losing money with every sale. You can learn more about the formula behind book pricing in the Launching chapter.

This is why I look at POD sales as bonus free money rather than making this the sole way I sell my books. It is a bonus because once the book is loaded, I do not have to lift a finger to print, pack and post my book, it is all taken care of for me. All I have to do is read the sales report when it lands in my inbox and eagerly await the money landing in my account. Look at it this way: a POD platform allows you to cast a much wider net that returns less in royalties, while your own website might have a smaller net with less reach, but returns a might higher profit margin.

Product platforms

Before you even consider why you would bother if the returns are so low, come back to your 'why'. If reach and accessibility are goals of yours, POD ticks all the boxes and is unrivalled at where it can get you online and even in stores if you market your book well.

So yes, while profit margins are slimmer, particularly if you're pricing your book competitively, this is often a fair trade-off for the convenience and minimal financial risk. The real value of POD lies in freedom, accessibility and control. You get to put your book into the world without needing a garage full of stock or a warehouse team on call. For many, it's the ideal first step and a way to publish professionally while still testing the waters. Thanks to platforms like IngramSpark and Amazon KDP, you can do it all with a global reach that was once only available to traditional publishers.

Just be mindful when using these services that pricing your book correctly is even more important. You will find more information on this in the Launching chapter.

IN THE KNOW: PROS AND CONS OF PRINT ON DEMAND

Pros

- You can print copies as needed.
- No need to store inventory.

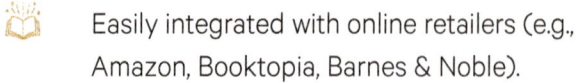

Ignite & Write: The Published Author

- Easily integrated with online retailers (e.g., Amazon, Booktopia, Barnes & Noble).
- Automatic order fulfilment and global reach.
- Fast setup.
- You can update or revise your book without reprinting thousands of copies.

Cons

- A higher per-copy cost.
- You have to print in all colour or all black and white, there is no middle ground.
- Fewer options for paper, trim size and finishes.
- Lower profit margins.
- Some retailers have slower shipping for buyers, as books are printed after purchase.

Ebooks

Once upon a time, ebooks were seen as the lesser sibling of print books – something extra you'd do *if* you had the time or *only* if you were tech-savvy. Fast forward to today and that perception couldn't be further from the truth. Ebooks have become a major player in the publishing world, not just for readers but for authors too. And if you're an author looking to expand your reach, increase your earnings and meet your readers where they are, ignoring the ebook format simply isn't an option anymore.

Product platforms

Over the past decade, ebooks have grown steadily in popularity.[13] Around the world, 364.28 books are sold each minute. Statistics show that in April 2024, US ebook sales grew by 16.8 per cent, making USD$83.1 million in revenue.[14]

> While print books still hold a strong place in the hearts (and hands) of readers, digital reading is no longer a niche activity.

From Kindle and Kobo to smartphones and tablets, millions of readers around the world are downloading, browsing, highlighting and bookmarking digital books because they're portable, instant, affordable and convenient. Think about the last time you went on a holiday or a commute. Chances are, your ereader took up a lot less space than a suitcase full of books.

For authors, the rise of ebooks is fantastic news because once your manuscript is written and edited, turning it into an ebook is a relatively simple and low-cost step, because the hard part is already done. Converting your manuscript into a digital format is just a matter of reformatting and uploading. In fact, most publishing platforms now walk you through the process, and there are affordable professionals who can do the conversion for you if tech isn't your thing.

Another massive benefit? Global reach. With just a few clicks, your ebook can be available in dozens of countries, on major platforms like Amazon Kindle, Apple Books, Google Play, Kobo and more. That means readers around the globe can discover and download your book within minutes. No warehouses. No shipping fees. No physical stock to manage. Just pure, borderless distribution.

Ebooks are also an incredible way to reach audiences who may not be buying physical books at all. Younger generations have grown up on digital devices and prefer to read on screen. Others live in remote areas where bookstores are scarce or shipping is expensive, and let's not forget people with vision challenges who rely on large fonts or text-to-speech functionality, both of which are built into most ereaders.

There's also the financial side to consider. The profit margin on ebooks is often higher than print, because there are no printing or shipping costs. While pricing can vary widely, many authors find success using ebooks as part of a launch strategy, offering early-bird or low-cost digital versions to generate buzz, build momentum and climb bestseller lists. Some even offer free ebooks to grow their mailing list or build an audience before releasing a paperback or hardcover version.

When we zero in on Amazon's services, they have Kindle Unlimited (KU) and Kindle Owners' Lending Library as subscription-style services. If you enrol your ebook in KDP Select (which requires exclusivity to Amazon for ninety days), readers can 'borrow' your book and you'll earn based on pages read, not books sold. Each month, Amazon sets a global fund, and your share of that fund depends on how many of your pages were read compared to others in the program. It's not a fixed rate, but for some genres, KU can be a solid income stream.

Product platforms

The key here is to think strategically. If your 'why' is to make your book accessible to as many people as possible, KU might work in your favour. If your goal is maximising profits per sale or having more control over where your book is available, you might opt out of exclusivity and sell across multiple platforms.

Adding an ebook to your publishing strategy is one of the easiest ways to amplify your message and expand your audience. It doesn't need to be complicated or expensive, but it *does* need to be intentional. Make sure your formatting is clean, your cover is optimised for thumbnail view (since that's how it will appear on screens) and your metadata (title, keywords, description) is dialled in to help readers find you.

So if you haven't considered going digital yet, this is your sign: do it. Your future readers are already searching online. Make sure your book is there waiting for them.

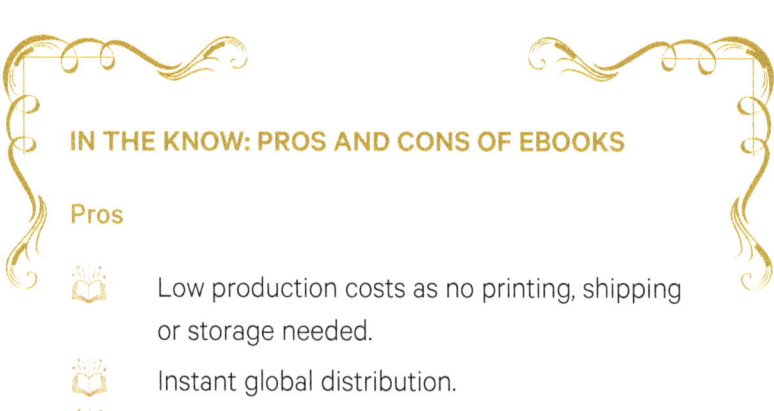

IN THE KNOW: PROS AND CONS OF EBOOKS

Pros

- Low production costs as no printing, shipping or storage needed.
- Instant global distribution.
- Quick to publish.
- High royalty rates with up to seventy per cent royalties on platforms like Amazon KDP.
- Environmentally friendly.

- Easy to update – you can revise or re-upload a file anytime if changes are needed.
- Readers can access ebooks on phones, tablets, ereaders or computers.
- Can be easily shared, promoted, or used for giveaways.
- A great way to gauge reader interest before investing in print formats.

Cons

- Some readers prefer print.
- With millions of ebooks available, visibility can be a challenge.
- Ebooks need to be properly formatted for different devices (EPUB, MOBI, etc).
- Ebooks are often priced lower, which can impact perceived credibility or value.
- They can be copied or shared illegally more easily than print books.
- Some regions or demographics still prefer or rely on physical books.

Audiobooks

Audiobooks are the fastest-growing segment of the publishing industry. Not so long ago, audiobooks were seen as a niche

Product platforms

product that people only used for long car trips or were suitable for those with visual impairments. But today they're mainstream and they're changing the way people experience stories and information. If you're looking to make your book more accessible, more profitable and more widely consumed, creating an audiobook is an option worth serious consideration.

The numbers speak for themselves. Global audiobook revenue continues to climb year after year and major platforms like Audible, Apple Books, Google Play and Spotify are investing heavily in audio content because listeners are hungry for it.

The year 2024 was a banner year for audiobooks, with the first ten months generating $883.4 million in revenue. The global audiobook market is set to grow to $35.05 billion by 2030.[15] This is because people are busier than ever and audiobooks allow them to 'read' while they're commuting, cooking, walking the dog, or even winding down at night. For many people, audio isn't just a convenience, it's their preferred or only way of absorbing content due to visual impairment or other challenges that prevent them from being able to sit for long periods or hold a book or tablet.

This is an exciting opportunity for us authors because creating an audiobook opens our work up to an entirely new audience that may never have picked up the paperback or downloaded the ebook. Just like ebooks, because the writing and editing processes have been completed, the content is readily available and ready for use. It is simply a matter of bringing it to life with your voice.

As with every element of your publishing journey, you can choose to learn everything and DIY, or hire the professionals to get it done for you. If you have a decent microphone, a quiet recording space and some patience, you can record your audiobook at home. You can do this with software like Audacity, GarageBand, Adobe Audition or Reaper.

There are even online platforms and studios that guide authors through this process, step by step, such as Soundtrap by Spotify or Descript. They are higher price points but offer more professional support. Of course, this space is always evolving, so do a little online research to find which is the best solution for you.

> I would highly recommend tapping into expert advice, as releasing an audiobook is a little more complex than simply recording your voice and adding an intro to upload.

The most arduous part of this process is the editing. You need to make sure every single word is clear and lines up with the words on the page. You also need to ensure you have the audio set to the right level and meet the guidelines set by the platforms, which dictate the maximum length of chapters and how to format the file to include the correct intro and outro information.

Product platforms

You could record yourself and then have it professionally edited, or go all in and head to a professional studio with a recording technician who can handle all the fiddly elements for you, so all you have to do is prep your voice and read.

Recording your audiobook in a professional studio with an experienced technician by your side can elevate your story in ways that DIY setups simply can't. A soundproof studio eliminates distracting background noise, while a skilled technician ensures every word is balanced, paced and polished for the listener's ear. They'll guide you through breath control, tone adjustments and even catch slip-ups you might miss. The result? A professional, immersive listening experience that reflects the quality of your work and builds credibility with your audience. You've invested so much into writing your book, this final step is about honouring that effort and giving your story the best chance to shine.

When it comes to whose voice to use, there are a couple of options. You can narrate it yourself, which can be fantastic because your book is nonfiction, personal and written in your own voice. Listeners love hearing from the author directly, particularly when it's a memoir, business, self-help, or any genre that benefits from authenticity and personality.

The second option is to hire a professional narrator. This is a great choice for fiction or books where tone, pacing and character matter. Professional voice actors bring a level of polish and performance that can take your book to the next level. There are platforms like ACX (Amazon's Audiobook

Creation Exchange), Findaway Voices and Voices.com where you can browse narrators, listen to samples and audition talent for your book.

If you choose to work with a professional voice actor, you could potentially negotiate a royalty share agreement. This means you split your royalties evenly, which can be a great option if you don't want to pay upfront for narration. Please note, though, that it will mean sharing your royalties in perpetuity and not all voice actors will enter into this type of agreement. I'm a fan of what my mum always said, 'You don't know if you don't ask'.

I would highly recommend plucking up the courage to narrate your own book.

I am a huge consumer of memoir and autobiography audiobooks, as they help me to keep up with storytelling trends. I am also just genuinely fascinated by people's stories. I listened to Deborah Feldman's *Unorthodox* around the time her book was adapted for a Netflix series. I wanted to listen to her full story before diving into a director's interpretation, and I really enjoyed the book.

When the sequel, *Exodus, Revisited*, came out, I was jarred because there was a different voice narrating the book. It was only then that I realised Deborah had used a voice actress for her first book and had chosen to read the second herself. You may not think that's an issue, but because you know I am such a stickler for establishing connection to your readers, guess what? I was more connected to the voice actress

Product platforms

because I associated *her* with being Deborah. She was my first experience of the story.

So when Deborah came along with the second voice, my brain told me that she was the imposter. Oh! The marvel that is the human brain. But these are very real considerations if connection to your reader is one of your main goals.

Sure, the idea of sitting in a studio reading from the pages of your book might make you feel a little squeamish, but believe me, the payoff will be worth it. When your readers meet you in real life, come along to a workshop or hear you speak on stage or in a podcast interview, they will immediately recognise your voice and that familiarity will serve you well.

Either way, once your audiobook is produced, distributing it is surprisingly straightforward. Through ACX, your audiobook can be published to Audible, Amazon and Apple Books. With platforms like Findaway Voices or Authors Republic, you can distribute to dozens of other retailers, libraries and even subscription services like Spotify and Scribd.

Audiobooks can be a smart revenue stream, but be aware that your royalties will depend on your pricing and platform choice. If you choose to distribute your audiobook exclusively through Audible, Amazon or iTunes, you will earn forty per cent of the net sales (that's the cut after the platform takes its share, not the full retail price). The upside of this is that you get a bigger slice of the pie, but the trade-off is that you cannot sell your audiobook anywhere else.

If having control and flexibility is more your thing, and you want to offer your audiobook on other platforms too, you can opt for non-exclusive distribution. That earns you twenty-five per cent of net sales, but you then have the freedom to share your work far and wide.

There's one more layer: if your audiobook is picked up in programs like Audible Plus or Premium Plus, you won't earn through traditional sales, but rather based on how many times your book is downloaded or how many pages are listened to. That can vary each month, so it's worth keeping an eye on.

The important thing to remember is this: your audiobook royalty structure should align with your 'why'. If your goal is to maximise reach, a non-exclusive path might suit. If it's about making the strongest return from a specific audience, exclusivity might be your best bet.

It's all about staying intentional with your choices.

No matter which route you choose, because there are fewer audiobooks available than print or ebook titles, discoverability can actually be higher. You're not just another title on a crowded bookshelf; you're one of a smaller group being offered to an increasingly eager audience.

Audiobooks also elevate your author brand. They help you establish a presence in multiple formats, make your

Product platforms

book accessible to people with reading difficulties or visual impairments and show that you take your work seriously.

Just like every other aspect of publishing, you can do it your way: DIY it, outsource it, or blend the two. I would recommend engaging a professional to record and produce your audiobook to save you a lot of headaches. Of course, there are rules you need to follow that govern everything from the pitch of the audio through to the length of each chapter. Additionally, there are specific requirements for how to begin and end the recordings to meet the standards accepted by audiobook platforms. Unless you are already across these (or are prepared to take the time to learn them), you'll likely save a lot more time getting the pros to handle it for you.

Then all you have to do is rock up with your book, some honey, a large water bottle to keep those vocal cords lubricated, and boundless energy to get you through the many takes for your book. It really is a lot of fun!

Distribution

There's something deeply satisfying about seeing your book propped up on a bookstore shelf, nestled among other titles, ready to catch the eye of a curious reader. It's the kind of moment that many authors dream of. But getting your book into retail stores, libraries and even specialty shops doesn't happen by chance. It happens through distribution.

Distributors are the gatekeepers between your book and the wider book-buying world. They act as intermediaries, bridging the gap between publishers (that's you, if you're self-publishing) and the retailers who sell to readers. When a bookstore or library wants to order a book, they usually don't go looking on author websites or Amazon; they go straight to the catalogues of trusted distributors.

You've likely heard of Ingram, one of the biggest and most accessible options for indie authors, especially because you know about its self-publishing arm, IngramSpark. If your book is available through Ingram's system, it becomes globally visible to more than forty thousand retailers, libraries and online stores. But IngramSpark isn't the only option.

For authors looking to go beyond POD or who are aiming for wider trade-level exposure, it's worth exploring traditional book distributors.

These are companies that work more closely with booksellers and often actively pitch titles to retailers. These distributors usually have long-standing relationships with national bookstore chains, independent bookshops, libraries and even non-traditional outlets like gift stores and airport retailers. Some may even have dedicated sales reps who visit book buyers in person to showcase new titles.

Here's the catch: traditional distribution is curated. These companies don't take every book that comes their way. They're selective because their reputation with booksellers

Product platforms

depends on the quality of what they represent. To engage a distributor like this, you'll typically need to present a well-produced, professionally edited book, as well as a strong sales and marketing plan. The icing on the cake will be your ability to showcase your momentum by providing early reviews, pre-order numbers or media interest that shows you're not just launching a book, you're building a brand.

Some examples of traditional book distributors that may work with independent authors or small presses at the time of writing include:

- Booktopia Publisher Services (Australia)
- Peribo (Australia/New Zealand)
- NewSouth Books (Australia)
- Independent Publishers Group (US)
- Consortium Book Sales & Distribution (US)
- Turnaround (UK)
- Gardners (UK/EU).

These companies often require you to go through a submission process, and if accepted, they'll handle warehousing, order fulfilment, invoicing and relationships with booksellers. In many ways, this model mirrors traditional publishing, except you retain more control and potentially keep a larger slice of the royalties.

It's important to understand that traditional distributors often require offset-printed stock, not print on demand. That means you'll need to invest in a print run and have inventory ready for warehousing. They may also charge storage or distribution fees and take a percentage of sales, so the financial model is different to the lean, low-risk POD setup. But what you gain is a higher level of retail engagement and sales potential, especially if your book fits a clear market niche or has broad commercial appeal.

No matter which option you prefer, there is a universal truth: your book won't sell itself. Just being available in a catalogue doesn't guarantee sales. Retailers want to see that you're committed to your book's success. That means marketing, building your author platform, collecting reader reviews and generating buzz around your title. You can learn tips on how to navigate these elements in the coming chapters.

It is also worth noting that some independent bookstores would prefer to stock your books on a consignment basis. This means they will take a small number of your books to stock in-store, but you will only be paid once the books are sold. They will take a fee for the sale, which could be anywhere from thirty to fifty per cent. Some have fixed fees while others are open to negotiation.

With most agreements, they will specify a period of time your books have to sell, and if they remain in store, you will be contacted to come and collect them so they can give another author a try. As this is a regular occurrence, the bookstores will already have consignment contracts, so be sure to read them through and make sure you are happy with the terms before you sign.

This can be a great compromise as it means the store is not out of pocket and you have the opportunity to be featured on their shelf. However, it does take some monitoring on your end.

Product platforms

I have done this with several bookstores and found it can be a real mixed bag in terms of outcomes. With some stores, I have been notified straight away if there was a sale and they would send payment through, but in most cases, I would have to follow up with the store to get an update and chase payment if there were sales.

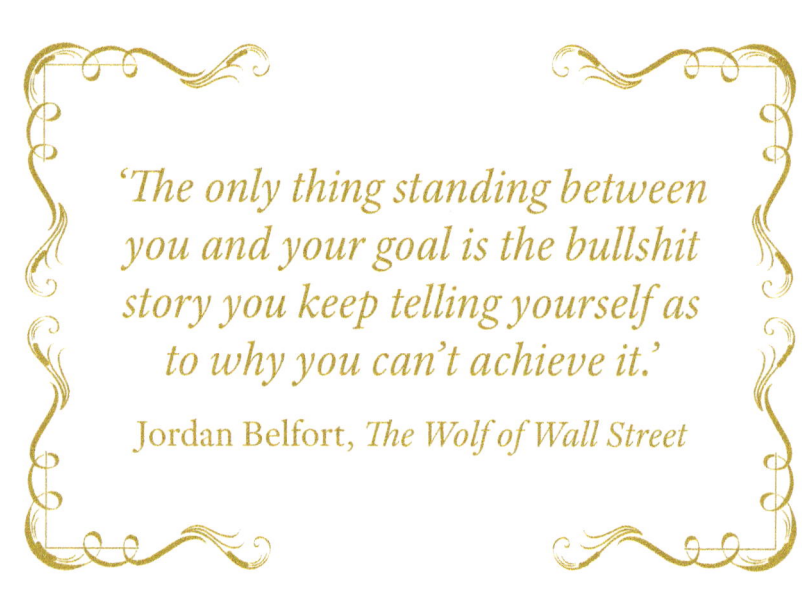

'The only thing standing between you and your goal is the bullshit story you keep telling yourself as to why you can't achieve it.'

Jordan Belfort, *The Wolf of Wall Street*

Marketing

All too often, I have watched authors throw themselves with absolute devotion into the process of writing their books, communicating efficiently with their publishers to assist the workflow as much as possible. They then launch the book they have poured their heart and soul into, with great expectations that people will come flocking from all around to get their hands on a copy. The only problem is, they didn't tell anyone they were writing a book. Or that it was being released. Or how to buy it. So what do they get? Crickets.

> Growing and marketing your book is the most often overlooked element of becoming an author. Ignore this at your peril!

Building your audience from the beginning brings people you may already know into the fold and gives you more of a chance to connect with those who can benefit the most from your story.

Even though your book may be a passion project or something you have wanted to achieve for personal reasons, it is beneficial to start to think of your book as a business. I get it, this can be a scary concept for some, especially if you have never run a business before. The good news is that it doesn't have to be hard work to get real traction.

The statistics are stacked against authors. NielsonIQ BookData reported that of 1.2 million books tracked, only twenty-five thousand – barely more than two per cent – sold more than five

Marketing

thousand copies.[16] But you know what? There's no reason why you can't be the exception.

Let me share the story of one of my ghostwriting clients – I'll call her 'Suzie' for this purpose. She is a prime example of how marketing from the early stages of writing your book will pay great dividends by the time you are due to release it.

Just before she started writing her book, Suzie used a social media platform to document her everyday life. Being a brilliant writer, she was able to engage people with her witty posts. Her audience grew exponentially as she managed the delicate balance between entertaining and educating people about who she was and what she was all about.

By the time the book launched, she had an incredibly warm audience (this is marketing speak for an audience who are almost ready to buy) of almost thirty thousand people from around the world. Of course, not everyone bought a copy. What did happen, though, is that Suzie barely had to do any traditional marketing because her audience was already there and waiting for the book to become available. She effortlessly sold her first print run of two thousand copies.

When speaking with marketing guru Joshua Clifton, the author of *The Hospitality Survival Guide*, on the *Ignite & Write Podcast*, he shared openly how marketing yourself and your book is a learning curve, but one well worth tackling.

> 'Marketing is so important and I think the biggest problem is that [authors are] fearful of it. Marketing is idea generation to product delivery. So, in essence, we're all marketers. If you're

writing books, you're a marketer. It's just that advertising prong that makes people a little nervous. And I think when we start marketing our book and ourselves, a lot of people have a lot of doubts. Like, *'why would anyone want to listen to what I have to say? Why would anyone want to do this?'*. And I say to them, 'Well, why'd you write your book? Is it just for you? Did you want to share it with people? What impact did you want to have?' And it's about sharing that journey and realising that it's not just about you, it's about your vision. It's about the message. It's about the problem you're trying to solve, or help, or assist, or leave with people.'

You can listen to the full interview here:

I understand a lot of authors are quite introverted and don't like the idea of putting themselves 'out there'. However, at the end of the day, people are buying *you* and they're buying *your* message. In order to get that into the world, you need to be prepared to step up and self-promote to build those connections with your ideal readers and get those book sales happening.

Grow an audience

I've mentioned this in both of the earlier books in this trilogy – it's never too early to begin building an audience. Imagine having a legion of fans ready and waiting for your book to be released so

Marketing

they can hand over their hard-earned money? Financial return may not be a key motivator for you, but you *will* want to get eyes on your book after putting in all of the time, money and effort to create it.

After all, what has all of this been for if not to make sure your book reaches the ideal reader you created in the first steps of your authorship journey? They were top of mind as you were writing and likely had a lot to do with how you structured and are planning to present your published work.

Allan Pease is an Australian body language expert and author or co-author of fifteen books. Allan and his wife Barbara have written eighteen bestsellers, including ten number ones, and given seminars in seventy countries. Their books are bestsellers in more than one hundred countries and are translated into fifty-five languages. In total, they have sold more than 27 million copies. But as he shared on the *Ignite & Write Podcast*, it wasn't all smooth sailing at the start of his authorship journey.

> 'We sold thirty thousand copies from the boot of my car before we even found a publisher. The publisher said, 'We'll print a thousand and see what happens', and I said, 'Bugger that, we'll print ten thousand and I'll buy whatever you don't sell'. That was the turning point. I went on every talk show, wrote letters to newspapers, handed books out on the street. I knew that to get noticed, I had to create the noise myself. If you wait until the book is out to start marketing, you're too late. You've got to warm the audience up months in advance.'

You can listen to the full interview here:

No matter which publishing avenue you have chosen, having an audience to market your book to will dictate its success. Those who put little effort into growing an audience before the launch of their book face a much steeper uphill battle than those who have taken the slow and steady approach over time.

Take a moment to think about your audience. Do you already have a strong social media following? Does your business have an extensive network or even an email list that you can tap into for marketing? Are you starting from scratch?

No matter what the answer is, if you start *now*, you can grow your audience of eager fans. You can build your audience through:

 Social media

Start to let people in on your process. Post up that you are starting your writing journey, offer them insights you've had while writing and how the process has been for you – the highs and the lows. Make it fun, make it real and make it uniquely you. They will begin to fall in love with you and your message, so by the time you are ready to launch your book, you will have people waiting with eager anticipation.

Some easy content ideas include:

Marketing

- Posting photos of your writing location.
- Talking about the fuel that is sustaining your energy levels, whether it is a block of chocolate (my go-to), a cup of coffee or a meal at a local café.
- Sharing cover design options and putting it to a vote (be prepared to have all kinds of opinions come out, be open to feedback, but don't be swayed easily!).

Don't be afraid to ask people to like and follow you. It's funny how simply asking for what you need is the only thing people need to be able to support you.

If you are finding it hard to build your following organically, you can also look at using strategies like hosting a competition, giving away a free signed copy of your book in exchange for people 'entering' by liking your post, sharing it and tagging friends they know who will love your work.

Be sure to make your contact details clear in your social media bio, so if people want to head to your website to learn more about you, it's just a click away.

IN THE KNOW: SOCIAL MEDIA PLATFORMS

If managing social media is new for you, don't be intimidated. Flip that mindset to realising this is simply a vehicle through which you can reach more people to tell them about your book.

Here's a quick breakdown of the major players and how you can maximise your impact on each. Remember, you do not have to use every single one. In fact, you will have better outcomes if you choose your favourite two or three and focus on those.

Facebook

- Users: ages 25 to 65+
- Best content to post:
  - Personal stories behind your book or writing journey.
  - Facebook Lives or Q&A sessions to connect in real time.
  - Shareable quotes or snippets from your book.
  - Links to blog posts, reviews, or purchase pages.
  - Reader testimonials and behind-the-scenes content.
- Organic reach tip: Use 'groups' or your 'author page' to build community and encourage

Marketing

interaction. Ask open-ended questions to spark comments and shares.

Instagram

 Users: ages 18 to 40

 Best content to post:

- Aesthetic images of your book (#bookstagram style), especially flat lays or lifestyle shots.
- Reels with writing tips, inspirational quotes, or behind-the-scenes shots.
- Stories for daily updates, polls and engagement stickers.
- Carousel posts for educational or inspirational content.

 Organic reach tip: Use Reels and hashtags wisely. Collaborate with influencers or other authors to increase visibility. Consistent branding matters here.

TikTok

 Users: ages 16 to 30

 Best content to post:

- Quick, snappy videos showing the writing process or book packaging.
- Opt for BookTok trends like #bookrecs, #authorlife, #spicyreads.

- Dramatic or emotional storytelling moments from your book.
- Reaction videos to reader reviews.

 Organic reach tip: Stay on top of trending sounds and hashtags and post regularly. Authentic, less-polished content performs well here.

LinkedIn

 Users: professionals aged 30 to 60

 Best content to post:

- Thought leadership pieces related to your book topic.
- Milestones (publishing deals, book launches, awards).
- Articles and insights drawn from your expertise.
- Speaking opportunities and behind-the-scenes from events.

 Organic reach tip: Post during weekdays and add value through education and insight. Use storytelling to connect your book to professional or business growth.

X (formerly Twitter)

 Users: ages 25 to 50

 Best content to post:

- Short quotes or thoughts from your book.

Marketing

- Hot takes, witty observations, or tips related to your niche.
- Participate in writing chats (#writingcommunity, #amwriting).
- Share links to longer content like blogs or podcast interviews.

 Organic reach tip: Tweet frequently, engage with others and use relevant hashtags to join conversations.

Pinterest

 Users: primarily women aged 25 to 45

 Best content to post:

- Quote graphics and visual snippets from your book.
- Infographics (e.g., writing tips, book structure guides).
- Beautiful pins that link to your website or book sales page.

 Organic reach tip: Focus on evergreen, SEO-rich pins and use Canva for design. Pinterest acts more like a visual search engine than a social platform.

YouTube

 Users: ages 25 to 50+

 Best content to post:

- Longer-form content like interviews, author vlogs, book trailers.
- Writing advice or tutorials.
- Read-alouds or sneak peeks from your book.

Organic reach tip: Use clear, searchable titles and thumbnails. Consistency and authenticity build a loyal following.

Threads

- Users: Emerging platform with Instagram-linked audience
- Best content to post:
    - Conversational text posts, short reflections or commentary.
    - Cross-promotion of Instagram content.

Organic reach tip: Jump on real-time threads and casual, human-first posts. This platform is still developing, so early adopters may benefit from low competition.

Goodreads

- Users: Book lovers of all ages, heavily reader-focused
- Best content to post:
    - Author Q&As and book announcements.
    - Updates on your writing progress.
    - Encourage reviews and ratings.

Marketing

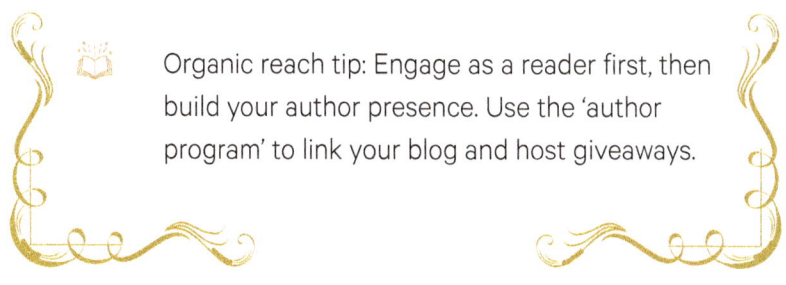

Organic reach tip: Engage as a reader first, then build your author presence. Use the 'author program' to link your blog and host giveaways.

Traditional media (print, radio, television)

You don't have to wait until your book is launched to start making yourself known, particularly in the realm of your subject matter. If something timely is being discussed on a local, state-wide or national level, there's no reason why your voice shouldn't be heard. Connect with the relevant media and join the conversation. The more your name and image are connected to your subject matter, the more recognisable you will become and the more respect you will gain as a leader on that subject. You can find tried and tested tips on writing media releases from this former journo later in this chapter.

Podcasts

Even if you describe yourself as shy, shedding that stereotypical introverted author personality will benefit you now. Why? Because it's essential to build your profile and promote your work to build an audience. You can either create your own podcast and build a community of listeners, or you can leverage someone else's community and appear as a guest.

Ignite & Write: The Published Author

There are so many reasons why podcasts are an amazing option to help you do this:

- You can do it from the comfort of your own home! Check whether the interview will also be filmed, and if not, you can even do it in your pyjamas.
- Podcasts expose you to new and potentially large global audiences that may not otherwise hear about your work.
- Being a podcast guest allows you to showcase your expertise and share insights, which helps build credibility as an author and thought leader in your niche.
- This is a platform through which you can connect with audiences on a personal level through storytelling in a conversational setting with your real voice. Have you ever built a picture of what someone looks and sounds like when you read about them all the time, and then been surprised when you see them in real life or catch a video of them? Podcasts allow you to remove the mystery.
- Regular podcast appearances can develop trust as listeners feel more connected to your personality and values.

There are millions upon millions of podcasts out there. Many podcasts focus on specific topics, so take some time to search for those that are in the top ten in your niche or genre and reach out to the hosts. Podcast interviews are often free or low-cost compared to other promotional methods, like ads, so you will be able to trade a little bit of time in exchange for tapping into the host's audience.

Marketing

Remember, don't just do the interview and forget about it. Share it with your audience on social media, in an email newsletter and also on your website; the more ears that listen, the more your message will get out there. Unlike traditional media, podcast episodes are usually available for replay, providing the potential for ongoing exposure long after the initial release, so make the most of it.

 Email lists

It is never too early to start collecting email subscribers. Early sign-ups are the most likely to be your biggest fans and most unwavering supporters. If you are in this for the long haul, I recommend using a high-quality email list management software so that your emails actually reach your ideal reader and don't consistently land in their junk or spam boxes. Sadly, emails from many of the free platforms are sorted as rubbish by email providers, so your emails may not even be seen.

Don't panic! You do not have to produce a newsletter every week. Just keep in mind that you should not be 'selling' something every time (and the only time) you contact your subscribers.

Place a sign-up form on your website or create a landing page you can direct people to from social media. All you need is their first name and email address – you don't want to scare people off by asking for more.

Consider including a sign-up incentive, like a promo code for your latest book, a bonus chapter, a sneak preview of your next book, or a free resource.

Videos

Whether you place them on your own website, on social media or start your own YouTube channel, visual engagement through videos helps you to become much more memorable than your average author. Better yet, you can repurpose content across all three to really leverage your work.

What sort of videos can you create?

- Share knowledge through tutorials.
- Record interviews or discussions with other experts in your field.
- Show behind-the-scenes content.
- Book trailers.
- Host live Q&A sessions.
- Vlogs that document what you are up to.
- Educational videos that cover one topic at a time.

At the time of print, YouTube is owned by Google, so well-optimised video content can improve search engine visibility, leading to higher discoverability. By transcribing your videos, you also have ready-made content that you can use for blogs, text-based social media posts and even scripts for podcast episodes.

Networking events

Getting out into the world and connecting with others can help you build a genuine, engaged audience that's excited for your story. Networking isn't about walking into a room and pitching your book, it's about forming relationships. Whether you're attending industry conferences, community events, writing

Marketing

workshops, or niche meetups relevant to your book's theme, these spaces are full of opportunities to meet people who could become future readers, collaborators, beta testers, or advocates.

The key is to show up with authenticity. Share why you're writing your book, what it means to you and who it's for. When people connect with your 'why,' they're more likely to follow your journey, spread the word and cheer you on when it's time to launch.

Networking also opens doors to speaking opportunities, guest blogging, podcast interviews, or media features, which are all ways to grow your visibility before you publish. Don't underestimate the ripple effect; the more conversations you have, the more connections you build and the wider your future reach becomes.

Bring business cards (or digital contact tools), follow up with those you meet and keep people in the loop as you progress. You're not just marketing a book, you're inviting people to be part of your journey.

Even if being around people is not your favourite thing, it's time to take a bold step and go to the events, talk to strangers, ask questions and share your passion. Every handshake or hello could be the start of a new reader relationship and the momentum that carries your book into the world with strength and support behind it.

Leverage your audience

You didn't write your book on a whim. You showed up with purpose, heart and likely more cups of coffee (or bars of chocolate) than you'd care to count. You carved out time you didn't have, battled imposter syndrome and poured your story or knowledge onto the page. That kind of commitment isn't just admirable, it's powerful.

This energy has transferred into the book you are taking out into the world. Yes, I love a bit of woo-woo and believe there is an energy to everything we do. This is why I'm doing my darndest to bring the fun back into authorship.

> When you lead with positivity and authenticity, your book becomes more than just words on a page; it becomes an energetic magnet.

Readers don't just want your story, they want the transformation, the support and the connection that comes with it. That's where your opportunity lies. When people are inspired by your story and you show them how your knowledge or experience can influence their own lives, they're far more likely to buy from you, work with you and advocate for you.

That's the heart of this formula: Inspiration + Influence = Income.

Marketing

You've already done the inspiring part; now let's explore how to extend your influence beyond the book and build meaningful revenue streams in the process.

It is a known fact that people don't just buy your product or service, they buy you. They buy your energy, your values and your story. They buy from people they know, like and trust. The beautiful thing about writing a book is that you've already let your readers get to know you. When you step out from behind the pages and into the world, you give them a chance to like and trust you – that's when the real magic happens.

This was a recurring theme in my interview with Kim McCosker, who knows a thing or two about how to take a book and turn it into an international bestselling sensation. Not only that, but she also went on to create a business empire off her book brand.

Kim is the founder of 4 Ingredients, now a formidable Australian publishing house. It all started with a simple idea. 4 Ingredients now owns the rights to all forty-one cookbooks, tens of thousands of recipes, images, videos, manuscripts and databases with the reach of millions. It is the publisher of cookbooks, ebooks, apps and the developer of a wide range of kitchenware. It has grown to become one of the most recognised and trusted food brands in Australia, with a reported one in seven homes owning a 4 Ingredients cookbook!

> 'Don't take no for an answer. If you don't at first get a publishing deal, then self-publish and market yourself. Because the game has changed. We ceased being authors and we commenced being marketers. It's not just about writing a

book anymore. It's about how you take that book and sell it, how you market it. We learnt how to write a press release and sent it to everyone we could think of – radio, TV, newspapers. Then we did something extraordinary: we followed up with a simple phone call. That phone call changed everything. Day after day, week after week, month after month, we were on the phone to media, retailers, bookstores. It was exhausting. But people resonate more with your weakness than your strengths. They relate to the story of the struggling author making thousands of phone calls trying to get their book out there. We rang each bookstore twice. The first time as a phantom shopper and the second time a week later as Kim McCosker, the struggling author, really appreciative of their support. That personal touch made all the difference.'

You can listen to the full interview here:

The message is simple. You can stay quiet and keep your story tucked away on a bookshelf, or you can choose to be brave and let your book become a beacon. Those who share, show up and speak their truth are the authors who get paid. Yes, it really is that simple. If you have a book that is the best-kept secret, no one is going to know you or your incredible message.

So how exactly can you leverage your book to create a sustainable income? The options are rich and varied, and the

Marketing

best part is you get to shape them in a way that aligns with your strengths, your message and your lifestyle.

To fully step into the business of authorship, you need to take things to the next level and leverage the audience you are building. Here are some thought-provoking ideas that might spark a new inspiration for you:

 One-to-one service

I started my business ghostwriting one book at a time. There are many ways you can offer a one-to-one or done-for-you service that links in with your book's themes. If your story is tied to a journey, transformation, or area of expertise, chances are there are people out there who'd love to work with you directly. Just remember, your time is precious. Price accordingly and deliver value with care.

 Workshops

This is a one-to-many model that's ideal for scaling your impact. These can be intimate, high-touch events or larger-scale sessions, depending on your goals and audience. I discovered that many people didn't want someone to write their book for them; they wanted the tools and support to do it themselves. Workshops let you guide and empower others without the heavy lift of doing the work for them.

 Group programs

To keep the momentum going after a workshop, you might offer a group mentorship or program. This is perfect for helping readers take what they've learned from your book and apply it with structure, accountability and community. Whether it's a twelve-week writing journey, a health challenge, a mindset reset or a creativity course, this is a brilliant space to serve while fostering deep connection and transformation.

 Speaking

Standing in front of a room, or even a Zoom screen, and sharing your story aloud is one of the most impactful ways to grow your reach and your income. Whether it's a reading at a local school, a panel at an industry event, or a keynote on a national stage, speaking builds trust fast and positions you as an expert. Yes, it can pay well. You don't have to start big, just start somewhere.

 Build a community

Another beautiful way to extend your influence is by building an online or in-person community around the themes of your book. Whether it's a free Facebook group, a paid membership, or a monthly meetup, communities create belonging. When people feel like they belong, they stick around, they engage and they invest.

No matter which path you choose (or which combination), your job is to keep showing up. Share personal insights and offer value so people can see who you are and what you stand for. The more consistent you are, the more magnetic your message becomes. Even if your book is still in progress, you can begin now. This is all part of building the foundation.

Marketing

You've already proven you can do the hard thing – write a book. Now it's time to do the *brave* thing and step into the spotlight and show the world the bigger picture of how you can help.

As you discovered in *The Structured Author*, your book can be a pillar rather than a product, so why not build something spectacular.

 Testimonials and endorsements

One of the easiest ways to add credibility and social proof to your book is to look at who you can approach to support it. You will see in the front of all of my books that I try to have at least half a dozen published authors who can back up the content of my books, either because we have worked together or because they are renowned writers and people value their opinion.

When reading testimonials, I like to know they are from real people. This is why I have chosen to include photos of the people who have given me testimonials. I also include their book covers, so readers can see they have produced high-quality books that may be similar to how they see theirs in the future.

Most of it is psychology, but by having the full package of written support and visual confirmation right up front in the book, you may have been put at ease knowing this lady knows what she's talking about. It allows me to really speak to you from within these pages, adding a valuable level of connection. It's no wonder that I have had great feedback from readers about this strategy, but it isn't the only way you can include testimonials in your book.

One word of caution I would give is to make sure those giving testimonials are *relevant* to your book's content. For example, if you know an internationally renowned tennis player like Rodger Federer and you are writing a book about your tennis career, he would be the perfect fit to endorse your book or write a testimonial. (Personally, I'd hit him up to write a full foreword!)

But, if your book is about how you survived a shark attack, even though Federer is undeniably someone who would grab people's attention, he has no authority in this field (that I know of) so his testimonial would fail the test of congruence – there's no connection between his field of authority and the subject of the book.

If you have people already in your orbit who fit the bill perfectly, it will make collecting testimonials and endorsements much easier. But if you don't, I encourage you to think blue sky with who you can approach.

Young author Lincoln Rawlins, who happens to be my son, was eight years old when he wrote his first book, *Sprout's Idea*, in 2022. After seeing how many of his favourite picture books had brief, one-sentence testimonials on the back, he wanted one for his book too. When we thought about who he could approach,

Marketing

he was very clear: Andy Griffiths, the bestselling author of the *Treehouse* series.

Andy lives in the same country, which was a bonus, and he had an affinity for trees, which fit with Lincoln's book perfectly, as Sprout is, of course, a seedling. Fortuitously, I had interviewed Andy a few years earlier while in my role as a journalist, but I never had his direct contact details as the interview had been set up through his publisher.

Undeterred, I reached out to him through direct message on social media. I have serious doubts about whether he remembered our connection, but he loved Lincoln's book concept and the fact he was so young and didn't hesitate to send through the one-sentence testimonial Lincoln had asked for.

This small action from an international author meant the world to Lincoln; it was as if he'd won $100 million in the lottery! The following year, Lincoln and Andy met for the first time in person. It was such a magical moment.

So, you could say we'd set the bar pretty high for when Lincoln decided to release his second book, *Super Sprout*, in 2024. Looking at who was relevant to consider for an endorsement of this book, he gave me two names: Chris Hemsworth and Dwayne 'The Rock' Johnson. It's about as blue sky as it gets, sending your mother off to track down two of the highest-paid superhero actors in the world to ask them to endorse a picture book!

But, we have a never-say-never attitude in our household, and I gave it my darndest.

I tracked down the names and contact details of managers and publicists around them, sent multiple emails to each of them and followed up. We even sent a package to the Sydney HQ of Hemsworth's manager, only to find out that he was on vacation in the Maldives for an extended period of time.

We gave it a red-hot go on social media, putting out a plea and tagging everyone in the hope we could start a ripple effect that would get their attention. We even approached charities the actors were affiliated with to see if we could create a three-way partnership where the charity would allow the testimonial and we could then donate a portion of book sales to the charity in perpetuity. Whenever you can create win-win scenarios like this, you will have more of a chance of success than just asking for an outright favour.

After a couple of months, we decided to move on to Plan B, connecting with children's book authors to see who we could get on board.

Lincoln created another shortlist and we got to work. This time, however, it only took a single unsolicited email to international sensation Jackie French, author of *Diary of a Wombat*, and just like Andy, she was all in as soon as she heard about Lincoln and his book.

Marketing

You know you've found the right person when it just clicks. Jackie sent through her testimonial and we agreed to donate a percentage of every sale of *Super Sprout* to her Wombat Foundation. Lincoln's illustrator, Cara Ord, even added a few cheeky wombats into the pages of the book to strengthen that connection.

IN THE KNOW: HOW TO GET TESTIMONIALS

Consider these three steps your guide to approaching people for testimonials or endorsements.

1. Identify your shortlist

Spend some time creating a list of people you would like to approach. They could be people who are already in your circle of influence, or strangers. Just remember the rule of congruence; you don't want to be pursuing people just because they are famous.

But if some of the people who come to mind *are* famous, don't hold back. Spend a few minutes envisioning the 'perfect' blurb and what it would look like on the cover of your book or inside the front pages. Then go for it!

Think about who:

- is a renowned thought leader in your industry.
- is a household name that everyone trusts on your subject matter.

- has benefitted my products or services and can give honest, articulate feedback.
- has lived a similar experience to yours.
- has published a book with a similar theme.
- is at the forefront of research on the subject you are writing about.

2. Collect contact details

Create a spreadsheet that includes the names of the people on your shortlist and conduct a search for their contact details. If you know them directly, simply add them in. If they are unknown to you, it's time to hit up the world wide web.

Search their full name to uncover personal pages, business links or even management contacts. Add all of them to your spreadsheet so they are in one handy place.

I also like to include sections in my spreadsheet to record the date I contacted them, whether there was a response, when I followed up and when a testimonial was provided. This can be invaluable if you have multiple people to keep track of. In fact, it's so useful, I've created a Testimonial Tracker you can download as part of *The Structured Author* resources here:

Marketing

3. Send a well-crafted query

Your query letter will make or break your testimonial campaign, so it's important to spend time on it. Here are some tips to remember as you draft and review it.

- Keep it short. It's likely that the people you are querying are pretty busy. If you send a four-page letter explaining your book and marketing in detail, many people won't even have time to read it. Try your absolute best to keep it to one page.

- Introduce yourself. If the people you are writing to don't know you, you'll need to let them know who you are and why you're qualified to write your book. However, no one wants to read a resume or long list of accomplishments; it can put people off.

- Why is it important? This is your opportunity to communicate the 'why' you established way back at the beginning of your writing journey. Capture this in a sentence or two.

- Connect to a common cause. This is where you can show why they are the perfect fit for your book. You can use the reason you selected them for your shortlist. (Don't mention the word 'shortlist', though. You want them to feel special and not like they are one of many potential options!)

- Be specific about what you want. Don't hint, rather, ask directly for a testimonial from those readers who enjoyed your book. Don't forget to mention that you may edit the responses for length, since some will send you much more material than you need.

- Set a deadline. It sounds counterintuitive, but you will get far more responses if you set a reasonable timeframe for people to write something for you. Try to give them at least a week, but if you allow them months, they will not see the urgency and may forget about it.

- Make it easy. Don't send your book with the query letter, as it could be overwhelming. Instead, ask them which format they would prefer to have it in. If you are reaching out before printing, the easiest format would be a PDF file of your typeset book. If you have already published, you can ask if they would prefer an electronic or physical copy to read through.

4. Follow up

Give it a few days before following up with each of the people you have contacted. If they decline, remove them from your list. Remember, there may be any number of reasons a particular person won't write something for you. Don't take it personally. They may be busy, on a deadline of their own, travelling, contractually bound to

Marketing

not take on any new endorsements, or their brother-in-law is your biggest competitor. You never know.

When Lincoln asked Australian comedian, painter, TV personality and prolific children's book author Ahn Do if he would endorse *Super Sprout*, we were informed by his manager that he thought the world of Lincoln and his concept, but he had never endorsed books penned by his famous buddies and therefore did not want to trump them all by putting his name to Lincoln's project. An interesting refusal, but I get it.

If they simply do not reply, keep trying every couple of days until you get a response either way.

For those who have agreed, send a gentle reminder two days before the deadline to ensure timely submission. It's much nicer than having to chase up once their due date has flown by.

5. Show gratitude

When someone sends you content you can use, make sure to thank them. This simple step, which can be forgotten in your excitement of having received something, can help you in the future if you'd like to contact that person again for a future book. One cool way you can do this is to send them a copy of the finished book with a handwritten thank you note.

Website

I have seen firsthand just how difficult it is for authors to sell their books without their own author website. I assisted an elderly gentleman, let's call him 'John', in 2022 with a book on his family ancestry. It was a work of art, something he had dedicated two decades of research to. John went down the bulk printing route and chose to sell direct rather than utilise POD.

The only problem is, no matter how many times I encouraged him to create an author website, John chose not to. When the time came to promote his book, John had nowhere to direct people to buy the book. He started out with including his bank account details for people to transfer money into for orders that were made by email, but the reality is that we live in such an instant world that potential readers were turned off by the hoops they had to jump through in order to get a copy – no matter how interested they had been when they first heard of the book.

I might be a different kind of old-school, but I struggle to trust any book, business or brand that doesn't have a website. There is a practical reason to have one; it makes things easy for your readers to get a hold of the very thing you created for them.

> Having an author website is critical, no matter which publishing pathway you have taken.

Marketing

You will notice that even though you cannot purchase books directly from your favourite traditionally published authors, they still have a home base site that becomes the hub in which their readers and fans can congregate to learn more about them and receive their latest news and book updates.

The functionality of an author site is different for a self- or indie-published author. It is your 'shop' as well as the best chance you have of making the biggest profit margin on your work. When you use your own website to sell direct, you cut out the platforms that take a percentage of every sale. Of course, you can also use it as a place to announce new work, post blog content that goes into more depth about your subject matter or simply touch base with your readers. Remember, it is all about building your brand – a consistent presence goes a long way, not just for this book, but for future projects, too.

No matter where you sit, an author website allows you to add another level of connection to your readers. As you are well versed in now, this will translate into a boost in sales when people feel like they truly know you and trust that your book is the one they need to read.

Even if you are active on social media or put in the hard yards of promoting your book in more traditional media spaces, operating without a website can become a hindrance that you may not be aware of.

Ever had a conversation with someone and they've just finished reading a book, but can't remember all of the information?

'Oh my gosh, it was *the* best book on marketing, but... I think the name was... no, wait. Yeah, it was something about being an author who is published, but I can't remember who it was by. Oh! It was Roxanne... McCarthy? There was more, but she had a really complicated last name.'

Because I have an author website, I can search for 'an author who is published + Roxanne McCarthy' and even though there is no proper title, nor my correct name, the first few search results lead you to my work.

If you type those search terms into a platform like Amazon, I am nowhere to be found. Because online book platforms have such vast catalogues, searches have to be much more specific to lead you to the books you are looking for. An online search engine is much more intuitive and can lead potential readers to your author website with greater ease.

Learning how to design a website and incorporate the 'must have elements' requires some skills. Some authors are able to get their heads around this by tapping into existing skillsets or even learning on the go with the myriad video tutorials available online to help you set up a basic site. But if that makes you anxious, you can always enlist the help of professionals. You can have a functional website without the bells and whistles created without too steep of an outlay.

If you have an existing business website, all you have to do is dedicate a fresh page to your book!

No matter how you go about it, remember it is equally as important to showcase you as the author as it is to highlight how

Marketing

great your book is. In many cases, your site may be your future readers' first impressions of you, so consider these elements:

1. Home page

The home page is your chance to make an impactful first impression. This is where people will get their first taste of who you are and what your book is all about.

- Your site should look clean and uncluttered. Less is more and white space is your friend.
- Choose larger font sizes and colours that are easy to read. Light fonts on dark backgrounds or minimal contrast between font colour and backgrounds are difficult to read.
- Pick one colour to be your 'action' colour. Whenever you want a reader to take action by clicking a link or subscribing, ensure you use that colour only for the link or button, and nowhere else.
- Get someone to edit your web content; the last thing you want is to have typos on an author page.
- Keep navigation easy and clear, so your readers can find the important stuff.
- Avoid anything unnecessary, such as animated backgrounds or music. If your site takes a long time to load or doesn't work on a mobile device, you will lose people.
- Keep elements consistent from page to page.

Remember, your site has to be compatible with different browsers and devices, so check how things look on multiple browsers, tablets and phones.

2. About/bio page

When running a series of workshops for business owners, I shared how your 'About the Author' page is precious real estate that many people overlook. This is because it is among the most frequently visited pages on any website. In fact, a study revealed that fifty-two per cent of people tend to visit an about page after they first land on the homepage.[17]

Why do they do that rather than heading straight to the shop to buy your book? Because they are checking for similarities. For connection. They want to know if they can see themselves in your core values. It is also where they start to form an idea of whether they trust you and are prepared to be influenced by you, and whether you 'get them' and can solve their problems.

Therefore, if you show the personal side as well as your professional side, your prospects are more likely to be comfortable buying from you. In contrast, if you have haphazardly thrown up a stock-standard page just to fill the spot the web developer told you to, you are wasting a valuable connection point for your potential clients.

Remember, back in the dark ages when the internet did not exist? Most transactions occurred only after a personal meeting. People were comfortable doing business after a talk with a sales manager or business owner because they could determine whether they had a connection.

Thankfully it's so much easier to connect with your ideal reader through the magic of the internet. Your 'About the Author' page is your opportunity to connect directly with your existing and potential readers by lowering the curtains a little bit and bringing them into the fold.

When crafting this content, make sure you answer the following questions:

- Who are you?
- What problem/s do you solve for your readers?
- Why is solving this problem important to you?
- What makes you unique?
- Do you have any qualifications in the area you write about? (This could be either professional qualifications or lived experience.)
- When did you start writing?
- Where are you based?
- You can also add in some personal details if you are comfortable with sharing some quirky insights into who you are at home. Maybe some special interests, talents, skills, etc.

Do your best to make it memorable. Strive to create a lasting impression in the minds of your readers so they don't forget you the moment they close the tab. People are far more likely to buy books from people they *like*, so you want your authenticity to shine through.

Hot tip: finish with a call-to-action. If you've created an about page that has hooked your ideal reader and they've made it to the end, don't leave them hanging. End with a call-to-action so they know how they can get more of you. Some examples include:

- Buy the book now.
- Schedule a call with me.
- Download my free [X].
- Sign up for regular updates.
- Grab your limited edition, signed copy now.
- Check out our full suite of products/services.
- Find out more about how we can help you.

Even a simple 'Shop now' button can work well. Remember, your about page is akin to a lead-generating machine.

3. Contact page

The last thing you want to do is make it difficult for your readers to contact you if they are inspired by what they see. You can do this a few different ways:

- Have a contact tab in your top main menu and also on the bottom navigation bar. Use this page to list your preferred ways to be contacted. If you hate taking phone calls, don't include your phone number.

Marketing

- If you use a contact form, make sure it's simple and you're only asking for the info you require to get back to that person. To save time, add a few questions that ask them to articulate why they are reaching out. Is it an inquiry about your books? Do they want to work with you? The more you can refine this at the first point of contact, the less time you will spend asking questions when you respond.
- You can also encourage your readers to get in touch with you via the social media platform you are most active on. The benefit of this is that you can boost your social proof by increasing follower numbers.
- Make sure you have a tick-box option that asks if people would like to join your mailing list. Growing your direct contacts is always the best long-term option, as you will know who your readers are and can reach them with any new books, products, services or specials.

4. Shop

Depending on what you have to offer, you may have a separate page where people can buy your books, products and services, or combine everything in one.

For books, include your front cover, an enticing blurb and clear details on purchase options, which could be either directly from a shop on your site, or through an online platform such as Amazon. If you are directing readers to buy only from Amazon, consider joining Amazon Associates, and you can be paid an affiliate fee for other purchases they make. There are a lot of terms and conditions to read through, but it's worth looking into.

5. A blog

If one of your goals is to increase your invisibility, you can establish yourself as an industry authority and thought leader by including a blog on your site. Websites with blogs get fifty-five per cent more traffic than those without because the fresh, additional pages of content you create are great for search engine optimisation (SEO).[18]

Entrepreneur Zoe Sparks, who authored five books, shared her marketing journey on the *Ignite & Write Podcast*. She found the combination of having a strong website, adding blog posts and attending events was the winning formula for catapulting her initial trilogy onto a global stage.

> 'So I have a website that sits behind the books… it tells you a little bit about the books and what they do. At the same time, I was very much writing blogs that I would put up once a week, that sort of shared bits and pieces. Someone said to me, 'You know, use snippets out of your book. You've already got all your tips, you can turn those into blogs and that will encourage your audience.' I've always promoted on social media. But I felt a lot of value came out of [taking] stands at business expos throughout southeast Queensland, and I promoted the books, talked about what I did and that basically made the books take off. You've got to put so much time and effort into the marketing. I could see the reach and I could see that it was working.'

Marketing

You can watch the full interview here:

The traditional blog format may seem old-school, but these written articles are as relevant as ever.

- You can entice your current and future fans with exclusive, unpublished content, inside information and downloadable extras, like sample chapters.

- By writing about hot discussion areas on the topic you've written about, you have the opportunity to link to other sites. Over time, people who follow you may start to hyperlink back to *your* site. These inbound and outbound links all help to increase your importance when it comes to internet search engines.

- You can allow comments on your blog posts so people can communicate directly to you – like your own personal social media feed! You can encourage interaction with your readers, and when they start responding to each other's comments, you will see the formation of a new community centred around your work.

- You can add important updates for your readers. For example, if your book focuses on accounting or law, whenever there is a legislation or regulation update, you can be among the first to cover it in your blog. This will further cement your status as an industry leader.

- You can add additional content and bonuses any time you want to. Your blog community will be eagerly awaiting news of what is coming next.
- Share your upcoming author appearances, speaking engagements or provide reflections on events, workshops, markets or anything you are doing with your book to show how you get out and about.

Think of a blog as your own personal social media. If you are already active on other platforms, look at how you can repurpose that content to present it to those who are interested in your work.

Media

Whether we're talking about good old-fashioned newspapers or cutting-edge podcasts, media exposure is a powerful way to boost your credibility, increase your visibility and build trust with potential readers who haven't yet discovered you. Best of all, many of these opportunities are free – you just need the courage to claim them.

Traditional media includes print, radio and television. Love it or loathe it, these platforms are still some of the fastest ways to get your message in front of large audiences with minimal effort once the coverage goes live. But here's the thing: the fact that you've written a book, while admirable, won't be enough on its own. The key to getting noticed is crafting a hook.

Marketing

Your hook is your unique angle – the story behind the story. What makes your book relevant, surprising, emotional, educational or timely? Even traditionally published books are marketed with a compelling hook. You need to think like a publicist and find the 'why now?' behind your message.

Once you have your hook, match it to the right outlet. You might adore breakfast TV shows, but if your book explores accounting tips for entrepreneurs, a business news segment on Sky or a podcast like *The Mentor* would be far more effective. Aligning your pitch with the right platform increases your chances of getting a yes.

Timing is another golden thread. Consider aligning your launch or media push with an existing awareness week or public event relevant to your book's theme. I didn't accidentally release *The Mindful Author* right before Book Week. I did it because I knew media across the country would already be talking about books. Riding the wave of what's already on the media's radar makes you more relevant and, crucially, more urgent.

Start mapping out the awareness days, holidays and national events that intersect with your book's subject matter. If your book touches on mental health, for example, Mental Health Awareness Month offers prime timing. If it's about parenting, look at school holidays or National Families Week. These dates provide the timely hook that journalists and producers love.

But don't stop at traditional media. The media landscape is evolving rapidly and non-traditional media is overflowing with opportunity. Think digital magazines, blogs, YouTube channels, livestream shows and podcasts.

There's a podcast for almost every niche you can think of, and many are actively seeking guests who can offer value to their audience. Being featured on a podcast not only allows you to tell your story in a deeper way, it also introduces you to a highly engaged and targeted audience that you didn't have to build yourself.

Online publications and ezines are also fantastic entry points. Many accept contributed content, meaning you can submit an article that ties into your book's message and get published without spending a cent. You just need to match their style, meet their deadlines and show up professionally.

That's why I always recommend having a few high-resolution images of yourself ready to go. When you're writing for a publication that doesn't have the budget to send out a photographer, having your own quality photos can mean the difference between being featured and being overlooked.

> Media exposure works because it builds something every author needs: credibility.

When people see you featured in articles, hear you interviewed on podcasts, or watch you on the news, it sends a message. You are not just an author; you are an expert and a voice worth listening to.

Marketing

I've personally been featured in both traditional and non-traditional media, and sometimes the best opportunities arrive unexpectedly – a last-minute contributor falls through, a podcast guest reschedules, or a callout goes out for a voice just like yours. The authors who succeed aren't always the loudest. They are the ones who are ready.

That means being prepared. If you do not have the budget to engage a marketing agency to contact the media for you, you can craft your own media release. Luckily, I know someone who has built a pretty strong career in the media. 😉

There is nothing better than free coverage! The thing is, you need a hook. Media often won't run a straight-up business story without the space being paid for – you need something juicy to catch their attention and show why it's relevant to their readers/listeners/viewers.

Once you have that in mind, you need to write a media release that makes it easy for time-poor journos to process all of the information quickly and efficiently. Ideally, for print, you want to send them something they can use with only a few minor tweaks because it will boost the likelihood of it being used when compared to something they have to write from scratch. And if you provide a print outlet with a unique angle that you don't share with anyone else, you are onto a winner.

The reason why so many businesses don't do this is because they don't know how to craft a great media release, so I'm going to show you that right now:

Step one is to write out the key details first to make sure your presser answers all of the questions: who, what, when, where, why and how. You do not want to leave readers with any questions by the end of it. Then follow this template to create your customised media release.

You can download an electronic version along with other *The Structured Author* resources here:

IN THE KNOW: MEDIA RELEASE TEMPLATE

MEDIA RELEASE

Date

Headline

The headline of a media release should summarise the key points, but be catchy, interesting and strong. It is designed to catch the attention and encourage further reading. Ensure you bold it.

Lead

Start with your town/city (i.e., Sunshine Coast). The lead paragraph is the key part of your media release. It is essential that your lead is punchy and has the story hook. Check that it includes all the vital elements. Who did it? What did they do? Where did they do it? When did they do it? Why did they do it? How did they do it?

Body

The paragraph under the lead should expand on the lead and be the point where you start telling the story. The body of the media release is important to prioritise messages from the most important to the least important.

Use short sentences and short paragraphs and always write in the third person.

Use quotes to make your writing more interesting, but remember all assertions and opinions must be attributed to a particular person.

The media are unable to use newsworthy assertions unless sourced, and they will often call to check on the quotes.

End

The last paragraph is the least important information and can include background information or summarise the essential background information about the organisation, event or person.

Always finish the release with **'ends'** so the journalist knows it has finished.

Contact information

Add for further media information contact: include a contact name, email, phone number.

Boiler plate (About)

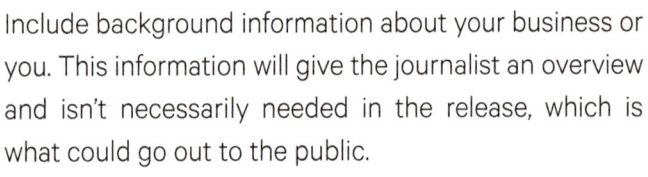

Include background information about your business or you. This information will give the journalist an overview and isn't necessarily needed in the release, which is what could go out to the public.

You can add your media release to a media kit (also known as a press kit). Think of it as your all-in-one toolkit that gives journalists, podcasters, bloggers and event organisers everything they need to profile you without the back-and-forth.

Your media kit doesn't need to be overly fancy, but it should be polished, professional and easy to access. A simple PDF is perfect, and I highly recommend making it downloadable from a dedicated page on your website. It's even worth printing a few hard copies to keep on hand at events or conferences, in case someone asks for one on the spot.

So what should a media kit include?

Marketing

- Your author bio – short, sharp, and full of personality. Include your contact details so they can get in touch directly.
- Professional author headshot – this is your face to the world, so make it count. You can also include action shots (e.g., at a book launch or speaking event).
- Book information – your back cover blurb, a few sample pages or chapters, and the book's key themes.
- A sample press release – especially helpful for launches or major milestones.
- Endorsements or testimonials – these help boost your credibility from the outset.
- Relevant links – to your website, socials, or online store.

Your media kit is like a warm introduction you've prepared in advance. It shows that you take your author role seriously and makes it a breeze for others to amplify your message.

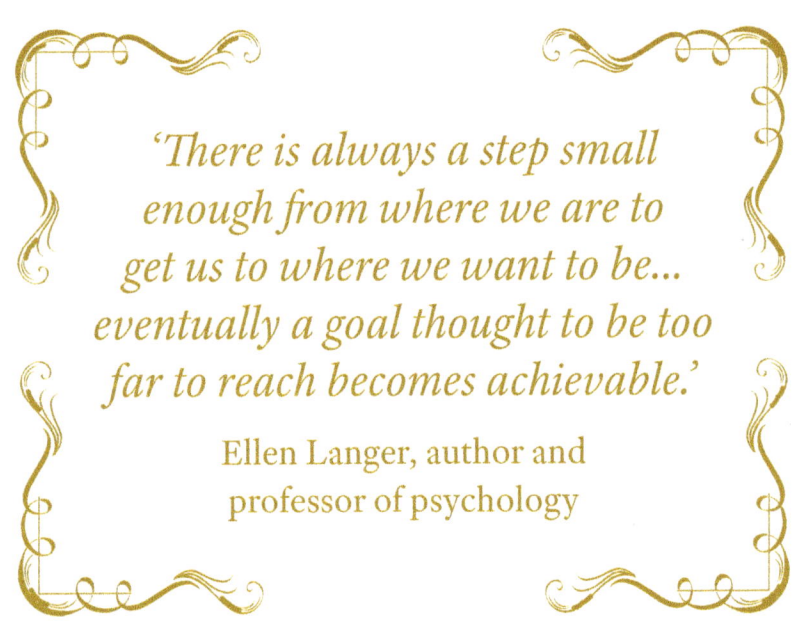

'There is always a step small enough from where we are to get us to where we want to be... eventually a goal thought to be too far to reach becomes achievable.'

Ellen Langer, author and professor of psychology

Launching

Your book launch is your first real chance to set your book free in the world and see it resonate with the ideal readers you created it for. This is something you can start to think about once you have begun editing as you know your book is now on the path to being released. I would recommend you really start to hit he ground running with the implementation of your launch plans once your book cover has been designed. This way you will have some visual capital you can use to generate some excitement!

I've been to many, many book launches in my life. Some of them have left me inspired, uplifted and feeling like I can take on anything I set my mind to. Others have left me yearning for the comfort of my pyjamas and bed because I'm trapped in a seemingly never-ending blow-by-blow account of every step the author took to create their book... then their designer's... then their publishers... and I'm past the point of intrigue and sinking fast into boredom.

It sounds awful because I know just how much goes into every single book that is written by a real human. But the fact is, your launch can and should be so much more than a sit-down talkfest about your book.

I get it, not all authors are even comfortable with stepping out from the anonymity of sitting behind the screen to stand on a stage – no matter what size – and put themselves *physically* out there. For some of you, this will be the first time you have done anything like this. So it's absolutely normal to be scared of the unknown.

But as Susan Jeffers says, 'Feel the fear and do it anyway'.

Let's look at a simple mindset switch here. Instead of looking at your book launch as a make-or-break scenario that will determine the future success of your book (oh, feel the *heaviness* around that) and flip that to become a celebration of what you have achieved with the book's creation and a chance to set it free to have a life of its own.

Like a child you have raised, you have nurtured this book, taught it everything you know, guided it with your lived experience and now, the book has 'come of age' and is ready to venture out into the big wide world. You do not hang off your young adult offspring while they backpack around Europe! No! You let them find their own place in the world, knowing you have given them everything they need to survive, make good decisions and have an impact in their unique way.

Your book is ready to pave a path outside of you!

Pricing your book

How much should you charge for your book?

It might seem like a small detail compared to everything else you've done to get here. But pricing isn't just a number on the back cover – it's actually a statement. It tells the world how much value you place on your work. It influences how readers perceive you, impacts your profits, your credibility and your reach. It can either support or sabotage your goals as an author.

For some, the dream is to sell thousands of copies and make a splash on bestseller lists. For others, the book is a calling card, an extension of their coaching, consulting or creative business. Your pricing strategy should reflect your intentions.

If your goal is wide visibility, especially at launch, you might consider a short-term ebook promotion. That magical $0.99 price point is not just a marketing trick; it actually works! It helps you drive downloads, get reviews and climb charts. But that's a short-term play, not a long-term pricing model.

When we do look at the long-term price, it's best to really think about buyer perception. If your book is tied to your business or your brand, you'll want to treat it like a premium product. Think of it this way: if you walked into a bookstore and saw a beautifully designed resource priced at $29.99, you'd probably take it seriously. If it were marked at $12.99, you might second-guess its quality. Price reflects value – and your story deserves to be seen as valuable.

Now, let's talk about the numbers behind the scenes. If retailers are buying through a POD service like IngramSpark, there are two essential things you need to know before setting your price:

1. The cost to print your book.
2. The retail discount required by the distributor, which usually sits somewhere between forty and fifty-five per cent, depending on the platform and territory. This

discount is like giving a wholesale price to a business that is prepared to stock your product on their shelf. In business terms, it's how the retailer makes their money because they will buy your book at the discounted rate, but then sell it at a higher price (which will hopefully be close to the RRP you have set, more on that soon).

Here's what that looks like in real terms: say your book costs $6 to print. If you set the retail price at $20 and give a fifty per cent discount to retailers, they take $10. Printing takes $6. That leaves you with $4 profit per book. Now imagine you priced it at $15 instead. The retailer still takes fifty per cent, which is $7.50, and your profit drops to just $1.50. Lower your price any further and you could be losing money on every sale.

That's why pricing isn't just about what feels right – it's about knowing your numbers. You should never, ever end up in the red just to move copies.

Luckily, with IngramSpark you can choose where to set the discount within their suggested range, and without hesitation, I will select the lowest – forty per cent – every time. Is it the smartest move? It may deter some retailers from purchasing my book, but the truth is, I make the majority of my sales direct to readers through my website and at events, so I see my POD sales as bonus money and not my main source of income. If you want to push more sales through your POD account, it is even more important to do the math when choosing your retail price.

IN THE KNOW: RRP AND WHAT IT LOOKS LIKE THROUGH POD

It is important to note that even though you can set your Recommended Retail Price (RRP) through IngramSpark and Amazon KDP, the emphasis really is on the *recommended*. When they push your book out to other platforms, each retailer has the final say over how much they want to charge for it.

This can be frustrating for some authors because they feel their readers are getting ripped off by these third-party sellers, and you could argue that indeed is the case. There are a few silver linings here:

- If you have a reader who is keen to buy your book and they find it for $59.97 on Amazon, only to go to your website and see it for $24.99, they are going to buy direct.

- You can make the fact that you have the best price on your website a marketing pitch. It's a great carrot to make more sales from your website, which means you are also getting their details and can connect directly to them in the future.

- No matter whether the retailer sells your book for twice as much or offers it in a half-price

Launching

sale, you will still be paid the same royalty (also known as author compensation) by your distribution platform.

So please don't let this get to you, it is just the way things are. Instead of firing off an angry email to Amazon, pop a post up on your socials comparing their price to yours and use it as an easy win to direct more traffic to you!

If you're planning to sell books directly through your website, at speaking events, or even out of your car boot (yes, that was a thing back in the day), your pricing flexibility increases. With direct sales, you only need to factor in the printing cost. So, if your book costs $6 to print and you sell it at $25, you keep $19. That's a beautiful thing. Even when selling through your website, readers expect to pay postage to receive their book, so you can make that element cost neutral.

I recommend going to the post office as soon as you get your test print copy to have your book weighed. You can then query the most economical way to post it nationally and internationally and use these as your postage rates.

Many authors find a balance between both worlds: selling via online retailers for reach and discoverability and offering direct sales at events for stronger margins and personal connection.

The key is knowing which route serves which purpose and making sure each sale supports your bigger picture.

One final piece of advice is to stand tall with your pre-sale pricing. Don't discount your book before it's even out in the world. Those early buyers are your champions. I recommend rewarding them with bonuses, not discounts. When you treat your book like it's worth the full price, so will they.

Planning the event

When my first book, *The Mindful Author*, was ready for launch, my then eight-year-old son had also completed his first picture book, *Sprout's Idea*. We looked at hosting two separate book launches, mainly because our ideal readers could not have been more different if we tried! But when we considered the logistics and the effort that goes into hosting an event and encouraging people to purchase tickets, we decided to go for something bold – a combined launch.

This meant our audience would have a mix of entrepreneurs, career-driven professionals, parents, grandparents and children. We had to be careful with how we structured the launch, and luckily, we had a hook – we were a mother and son who were stepping out as debut authors simultaneously.

I'm also not someone to take things too seriously. We chose to launch our books in August, which happens to be our birthday month, as well as when Australia's Book Week is held. Instead of

Launching

making it a bookish launch, we made it a party. A legit party. With cake, treasure hunts, giant dice and block building competitions. It sounds like a random hodgepodge, but everything was tied to themes of our books.

- *Sprout's Idea* begins with the birthday of the main character, Sprout – *cake*.
- When I work with aspiring authors, I remind them from the get-go that what they are creating is more than the realisation of a dream or completion of a passion project, it's a pillar on which they can build anything to help them make more money – *chocolate coin treasure hunt*.
- When the trees need to overcome the villain in *Sprout's Idea*, they make a ladder into the sky by climbing on top of one another – *block building competition*.
- You can choose to 'just write' and roll the dice when it comes to your writing, or you can have structure and direction to help you focus your efforts – *giant dice*.

See how we were able to put a fun twist on themes that mattered to us and engaged our audience at the same time? This is what makes book launches memorable. Of course, we did share our respective writing journeys one at a time and gave people a glimpse into what they would find inside the pages. Our Q&A was broken up by games that got our audience out of their seats and brought them into the action.

Ignite & Write: The Published Author

> The best form of flattery was seeing people who attended our launch then replicate the atmosphere with their respective books in the following months.

I know not every book's theme will lend itself to such a vibrant book launch event, but rest assured, there are still ways you can engage with your audience without party festivities. Paula Gowland launched her memoir *Legless*, which documents her story of becoming an amputee and the impact it had on her and her family physically and emotionally, and while the completion of her book was something to celebrate, she chose a much more thought-provoking approach.

For her activity, Paula created a whole whiteboard filled with notes that contained inspiring quotes from her book. During the break in her author interview, she invited everyone to go to the board and select a note that was meaningful to them.

It was interesting to watch how different people approached this; some read every single note until they found 'the one', while others simply let fate decide and grabbed one at random so they could marvel at the impact of the message chosen for them. It was a simple yet meaningful activity that further connected the audience with Paula and the overarching message of hope she builds on in her book.

Launching

When the time came for Lincoln to launch his second book, *Super Sprout*, we went all in on the family-fun approach. As his character is a small seedling, we found the perfect venue in Amazeworld, which features a deck overlooking a huge hedge maze (a nod to the main characters being trees) and many different puzzle areas and playgrounds that we were able to utilise for a Hero Quest.

We structured a series of mini quests, like finding your way to the centre of the hedge maze, completing a rope puzzle and doing two rounds of a small obstacle course on the playground, and had a responsible adult at each station ready to stamp their Hero Quest card to show it was complete.

Once they returned to the main deck with their fully stamped card, the kids received special raffle tickets and went into the draw to win some awesome prizes. This quest was the perfect way to balance out the beginning of the night, which was a fifteen-minute Q&A with Lincoln on the main deck to talk about his writing experience and share more about *Super Sprout* with the audience.

The excitement around being given permission to run amok with purpose brought the energy right up, and the whole venue was full of giggles and cheers as everyone got their stamps and raced back for their tickets.

When you can find something that provides your launch attendees with an unforgettable experience, they will be more connected to your book and it will stand head and shoulders above the rest as they have created positive memories.

Ignite & Write: The Published Author

IN THE KNOW: THINGS TO CONSIDER THAT WILL MAKE YOUR BOOK LAUNCH MEMORABLE

 **If you can, choose a venue that has meaning**

The launch of Margaret Sinclair's *Talinga: The House That Dad Built and its role in saving K'gari* was appropriately held on K'gari itself at the World Heritage Discovery Centre, Kingfisher Bay. This is a location closely connected to Margaret's narrative. Talinga, the house her father constructed at Eurong in the 1960s, played a significant part in shaping many pivotal moments in their lives. Additionally, the Discovery Centre features a tribute to her brother, John Sinclair, whose leadership in environmental conservation, particularly his efforts to end sandmining and logging, was instrumental in achieving UNESCO World Heritage status for the island.

 Think of ways to bring in your personality

Are you also an artist, musician or have some other talent up your sleeve? Put it on show at your book launch! Find a way to tie it all together and this event will be as authentically you as it can possibly be. When Angela Williams launched her book *Extravagant Life to Extravagant Love*, she wore the most

Launching

amazing red princess gown and paired it with work boots. This was the outfit she wore on her book cover as a visual representation of the dichotomy of growing up as the daughter of a British Lord and then founding a charity to support and better the lives of drug-affected prostitutes.

Maximise the theme

Leah Polwarth, the author of *Letters to Billy*, chose to have her book launch at the same venue where she used to work and where her late husband regularly performed. In an even more beautiful twist, she chose to host the launch on her late husband's birthday so she could make it a celebration of him rather than focus on his loss.

Cater for your ideal reader

If your ideal reader wouldn't like a big, showy book launch, you can have just as great an impact by having a small, intimate gathering. When Alex Gerrick launched his second book, *A Season of Thunder*, he chose to have two separate launches: one in Brisbane and the other in Canberra. This served him in two ways. Firstly, he was able to divide his launch party attendance numbers in half and create a more intimate experience at each one. Secondly, he could maximise attendance of the people

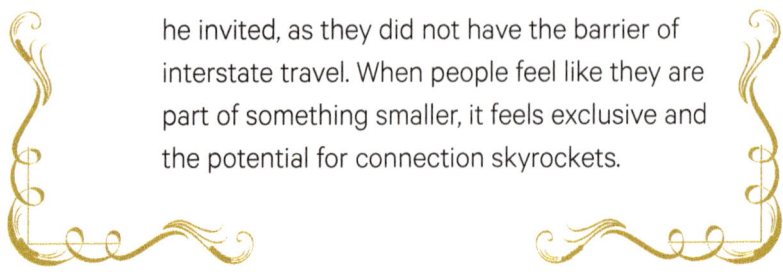

he invited, as they did not have the barrier of interstate travel. When people feel like they are part of something smaller, it feels exclusive and the potential for connection skyrockets.

Approach the planning of your book launch as you would with any event. These steps can help guide you through the process:

1. Secure a venue and date for your launch.

Remember, it is important not to rush your publishing process. I have seen far too many authors become attached to a particular date for their launch that may not allow the publishing process to unfold at a natural pace. Unfortunately, all this does is put pressure on the publishing team and the author as they struggle through each step.

Tight deadlines also remove any margin for error. I have watched authors reluctantly go to print with book covers they do not love simply because there was no time left to make the last remaining adjustments. You can imagine how something like that would take the shine off the whole book launch experience.

Once you have the venue secured, ask for a mudmap so you can see how everything will be set out on the night. This will allow you to plan where other elements, like your signing table, can go.

2. Book in any supporting speakers or entertainment

If you know you want to have guest speakers who have either contributed to the creation of your book or who are renowned in their industry and will add credibility to your book launch, get onto them the moment you have secured your launch date. This will give them ample notice to not only ensure they can make it, but also to prepare something meaningful to share with your audience. You may want to add some form of live entertainment like an acoustic performer, face painter, artist for live art, a wildlife carer to bring in animals pertaining to your book topic... there really are no rules! Note: If these elements cost you money, be sure to factor them into your ticket price when you move on to step three.

You may want to invest in having a professional photographer or videographer come along for the night. This would be especially useful if you wish to use your book for business purposes, as it will provide you with social proof and invaluable marketing content that you can tap into for months, even years, into the future.

3. Set your ticket prices

'Who pays?' It's a common question I am asked by authors preparing to launch their books. It's an important thing to consider as book launches come with expenses. This is one of those occasions where there is no right or wrong answer, only what is best for you.

I have been to book launches where the author has hosted a backyard gathering of friends and family, put on bubbles and nibbles and had a table of books on display for people to purchase. The pro for this is that there is no barrier to entry and anyone can come along. The con is that not everyone will buy a book and people will leave without ever seeing what you spent months, if not years, creating.

I have also been to launches where the author has paid for a full sit-down two-course meal for everyone and also given them copies of the book to take home for free when they leave. The pro for this is that everyone gets to see and read your book, which may lead to book reviews and other supporting advocacy for your book. The obvious con for this is that the author bears the full expense for all of it and loses the opportunity to make sales from their most avid supporters, who *would* support them if given the chance.

I prefer a model where your book launch becomes cost-neutral. This means whoever comes along pays their own way *and* you can build the cost of printing your books into the ticket price, so you aren't out of pocket. People who are willing to pay to attend your launch are also more likely to continue to support you through either future book purchases or by buying products or services you have on offer.

So, how do you make it cost-neutral?

It is as simple as working out the cost per head. You have to consider all of the relevant costs for your launch:

    venue hire

    food

Launching

- beverages (I prefer the 'one drink on entry then cash bar' approach.)
- additional entertainment if using musicians, performers or face painters, etc
- book printing
- signage or any other publicity material
- Decorations. Many venues include some level of decoration as standard, so see if you can make that work for you rather than adding to expenses. If you do have to jazz up the space a little, think outside the box on how you can create decorations that are also functional. For example, centrepieces that feature a few copies of your book stacked on top of one another with a candle or quote card on top. (This is where I get the most joy out of launch events – serving something unexpected that gets people talking!)

When you add all of this up, you can divide it by your expected number of people and that becomes your ticket price. If you want to make a profit and the cost price is reasonable enough, you can add a margin on top. Just be mindful of who your ideal reader is so you ensure you aren't setting the price at a level that makes it unreachable for them.

I found great success with my event by offering a mix of ticketing options to increase the value when people buy more than one ticket. This can be done by creating packages. For example, if an adult ticket is $45 and includes a copy of your book, which costs $9 to print, you can offer a couples package where the second adult ticket is $36 as it does not include a copy of the book. This makes it attractive for people to bring a friend or partner along, which boosts your audience numbers.

You could offer a low-priced child ticket if your venue offers a child menu option, such as nuggets and chips, in place of the cost per head for canapes for the adults. This now makes it an easy decision to bring the children, as the cost for them would be substantially lower.

There is potential to take this further by offering a family ticket. Using the same principle of one book per family, you can reduce the cost of two adults and two children by $27 (three $9 books) straight away. With a full-paying adult, a book-free adult and two children with $15 nuggets and chips meals, you could then offer a family ticket for $111. This is a substantial saving from the $180 a family of four would spend if each ticket was set at the full $45 each.

This makes it easier for people to feel like it's great value to bring the whole family rather than just book for themselves. Remember though, this strategy would not be useful if your book covers mature content that you don't want small ears to hear.

4. Create an event page to sell your tickets

It is important to have a central location you can direct traffic to when they ask how they can get tickets to your launch and there are many ways you can provide this:

 Create a social media event page.

Launching

- Build a simple landing page through your client relationship management system (CRM) or email software.
- Build a dedicated page on your website.
- Utilise a third-party platform like Eventbrite or Humanitix. Ensure your event page has all of the details you need to encourage people to come to your launch, including:
  - What is your book about?
  - Why did you write it?
  - What's in it for them if they read it?
  - When will the book launch be held?
  - What is included in their tickets?
  - How can they purchase tickets?

Make it visually engaging with photos, your book cover and other relevant imagery to make it stand out and add another level of connection.

5. Get the word out!

Use the strategies from the Marketing section to spread the word far and wide to attract as many of your ideal readers as possible.

6. Create a runsheet

You know I love a good plan and having one in place is super important for your book launch. You don't have to go to the extremes of plotting out every single minute, but definitely blocking out chunks of time for each element will help keep you on track.

With a runsheet in place, everyone will be on the same page, and you can share this with your venue managers, caterers and other volunteer helpers so you won't have the sole burden of running everything yourself.

Build in components like:

- guest arrival/check-in and mingling
- official start
- speakers
- entertainment (if having any)
- times for canapes/meals/snacks to be presented
- activities (if having any)
- thank you speeches
- any other special elements you want to include.

7. Gather assistance

Don't be afraid to ask people for help. It's the little things that can really mount up and make it exhausting if you try to do everything yourself. If someone offers to help, you can consider delegating any number of tasks to them. These include:

- checking people in at the door
- showing people to their seats (if allocated)
- preparing goodie bags
- decorating the venue

Launching

- collecting items for launch night
- keeping things running on time
- being the event MC.

8. Ensure your books are ready

I have seen too many instances where it has come down to the wire to have books ready for the launch. This won't be you if you follow my advice in Step 1, but if it is, keep in constant contact with your publisher or printer to make sure that you scoop up those books as soon as humanly possible. I have been to a book launch without books before and it's awkward for everyone.

For those of you who are organised and followed my advice in Step 1, you can pre-sign your books so you don't end up with a hand cramp on the night or a long line of people waiting for you to sign their books in person. Believe me, the novelty wears off quickly!

If you are including a copy of the book with ticket purchases, you will know how many to prepare. You can either sign your name and add a generic message so that the person checking everyone in doesn't have to spend time matching personalised copies to every single person. Or you can go all in and write personalised messages for those who have pre-purchased books with their tickets. I have seen this successfully done with meticulously laid out gift bags that are labelled on the outside and arranged in alphabetical order. It's up to you how far you want to take it! Either way, by pre-signing, only those who crave a personalised addition to their book will approach you on the night, leaving you free to interact with your guests and not be stuck at the signing desk.

9. Pre-event preparations

Preparation before the big night will help everything run smoothly.

- Create a banner that you can use for the launch and any future events you have with your book. These can be done cost-effectively through any printing services. Pull-up styles are the most popular, but I sprung for a full-on media wall backdrop style that has served me well as an eye-catching backdrop for markets and other events I have attended as an author.
- Once ticket sales have closed, print out a few copies of the guest list. Have two available at the check-in counter (you don't want to feel the stress of your only copy going missing) and keep one handy for your records.
- Make gift bags.
- Pre-sign books.
- Load up the car with decorations and everything needed for the venue.
- Contact your venue manager to finalise any last-minute details.
- Check in with entertainment or speakers to make sure they have everything they need.

Launching

- Prepare any slides, videos, photos or other elements you want to showcase on the night.
- Be sure to have a table dedicated to your book that allows people to purchase extra copies. This means having a payment option set up and available. (I always have a cash float and my trusty Square, which allows tap payments by card).

10. Enjoy the launch!

If this all sounds too much, you can always engage a professional event management or even a niche book launch service to do all of the heavy lifting for you.

While I highly recommend a book launch so you can leverage the hype of releasing your book baby into the world and actually celebrate your accomplishment, it is not a necessity. I would highly caution that if you choose not to host a book launch, you channel that time and energy into getting visible on as many of the marketing platforms as possible so you can create waves of awareness in that way instead.

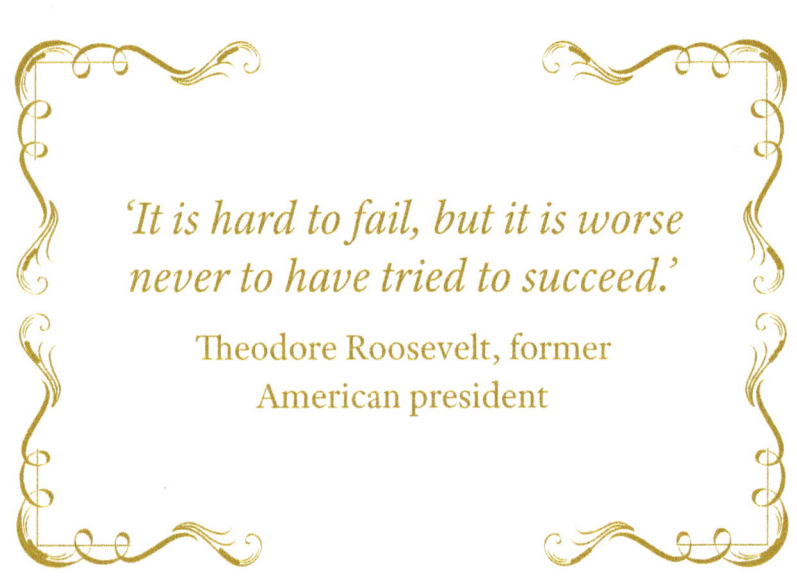

'It is hard to fail, but it is worse never to have tried to succeed.'

Theodore Roosevelt, former American president

The bestseller

Ignite & Write: The Published Author

'What does it even mean to be a bestseller?' This is a huge point of confusion for many first-time authors, although the allure of making it onto the bestseller list drives so many people. But gaining 'bestseller' status is not as straightforward as it may seem. In fact, many people scoff at the idea of it now because there are dozens of bestseller lists and each of them has their own rules for making the cut.

I'm sure you've heard of *The New York Times Best Sellers* list. It remains the most prestigious at the time of writing. But there are many others, including the *USA Today* bestseller list, the *Wall Street Journal* bestseller list, Amazon bestsellers, Barnes & Noble, *Publishers Weekly* and many other smaller platforms.

Traditionally speaking, you needed to sell anywhere from three-and-a-half to seven thousand copies in your first week to make a bestseller list. But some require a more modest one thousand copies sold, while others have needed ten thousand or more. It all depends on the platform and how exclusive the list is. For example, anything on *The New York Times* and *Wall Street Journal* lists must be traditionally published, which discounts all self and indie titles.

My books have made it as Amazon and Barnes & Noble bestsellers, but while it can give you bragging rights, those in the know understand that these are two of the easiest platforms to reach bestseller status on. For some authors, this is the pinnacle of success, and everyone's definition of success is subjective.

To make Amazon's main bestseller list, your book must sell at least three-and-a-half thousand copies in its first week.

The Bestseller

However, to make it onto the more exclusive Top 100 list, you'll need to sell around five thousand to six thousand copies. You can, however, gain a bestseller badge for being the top seller in your niche category. These stats change from day to day, and a book that has the number one status can be toppled from that ranking in a matter of hours, making it an extremely fickle platform to dominate.

Alex Gerrick's experience of watching *A Season of Thunder* climb steadily through the ranks over a few days to reach sixty-three in the Top 100 of all Amazon books in the Military Fiction category before dropping out again within a week following his first launch in Brisbane is not uncommon. The book then soared again after his second launch in Canberra to number one in the World War II History and 20th Century World History categories. I quipped that it was like watching the stock exchange, but this also shows the importance of marketing consistency to ensure your book stays relevant.

Pre-sales can be a powerful way to help boost your ability to reach bestseller status, particularly on the smaller platforms, as it boosts the number of sales you have within a weekly timeframe.

Pre-sales

A pre-sale is a great way to generate buzz and get people excited about your book. This is where all the prep you have done to build your audience pays dividends.

If you are working with a trade publisher, they will have all the launch and pre-sale details organised for you. But if you have chosen to self-publish or indie-publish, this will fall on you to organise. Do not be intimidated; it can be an easy process once you know the steps to take.

Pre-sales have many advantages, including giving your audience the opportunity to get excited about the pending arrival of your book and adding some much-needed funds to the coffers to help you with printing your books.

Here are some tips to maximise your book pre-sale exposure:

Let your existing fans and followers know

Yes, the common theme here is leveraging your audience. Let them know through social media, email marketing and even good old-fashioned word of mouth that your book is coming out. Share snippets of your book by reading a paragraph or two to pique your readers' interest and give them a peek at your cover design. There are many ways you can engage with your ideal readers.

Create a landing page

As you know, this is the easiest way to centralise all the information potential readers need, collect email addresses for future marketing efforts and take payment for pre-sales.

Offer a pre-sale incentive

Some of the more popular ways to encourage people to buy early are to offer something like a discount or free shipping on pre-orders. I recommend steering clear of discounts because it devalues your book right off the bat, *and* your first buyers are often your biggest cheerleaders and won't worry about paying full retail. Instead, look at a value-adds such as exclusive content or free chapter sneak peeks. If you want to take it up a notch, you can enter anyone who pre-orders into a giveaway for a gift card or more valuable prize, invite them to an exclusive Q&A, or create a swag pack that includes products or services you also offer. Remember, no one gets excited about a cheap cardboard bookmark, but they will climb over each other to gain access to an exclusive workbook, promotional events or a free online course. Think about how this incentive can help fulfil another need for your ideal reader.

Utilise other people's followings

See who has a following made up of your ideal readers and approach them to review your book. You can look at book bloggers, booktubers, social media influencers, industry thought leaders or anyone with a sizeable online following. Approach them with the clear directive to review your book, as if it is something they need to know about. When they give you a shoutout, it could mean hundreds or thousands of new eyes on your book.

In fact, you may choose to focus solely on collecting email addresses rather than pre-selling your book if you think it would be more beneficial to market to your audience when they can 'buy now'. All you would need for this is a landing page where you can capture email addresses. If you call it something exclusive, like your 'VIP waitlist,' and again, offer some kind of incentive, you can have just as much success with this to build your ability to directly communicate to your target market.

Let's look at Amazon for a pre-sale example. Amazon KDP is where the vast majority of self-published books are sold. At the time of writing, it controls as much as eighty-three per cent of the ebook market.[19] As with any good business, Amazon's main objective is to generate revenue and profit for itself and it does this by offering customers books they are likely to be interested in.

If you can show Amazon that your book is something people want to read and review, Amazon will help get it in front of people's eyes by ranking it higher in organic search results. Here's the kicker: pre-sales are added to your first-week sales. If you can maximise the number of people who pre-order your book through Amazon, you will get a healthy kick when your launch date comes around and all of those books are released and officially counted as sales.

IN THE KNOW: BESTSELLER TACTICS FOR AMAZON

When you list with KDP Select, you agree that you will list exclusively with Amazon for the first ninety days of release and this allows you to access a number of features that can help boost your book rankings.

The bestseller

To increase your chances of getting that 'Number 1' badge, consider the following ideas:

 Lower launch pricing

Launch your ebook at a price point like $0.99. This will encourage people to grab it while it's hot. This also allows them to also leave verified reviews. You can then raise the price to your RRP once you feel this tactic has done its job.

 Book reviews

According to the Spiegel Research Centre, products with at least five reviews are two hundred and seventy per cent more likely to be purchased than those without available reviews.[20] Send advanced reader copies (ARCs) to influencers, bloggers, or your launch team to get early feedback and reviews. I have seen strategies where authors have set a future launch date for paperbacks and opened up pre-orders with communication to their following that once readers have provided them with proof of purchase, they can receive epub or mobi files to read the book before it becomes officially available. The condition is that they leave a review the moment their official copy is released by Amazon. This spike in reviews sends a message to Amazon that your book is getting engagement and is worthy of promotion.

Utilise Amazon advertising

With KDP Select, you have access to a range of tools that allow you to advertise through Amazon. This is a marketing strategy that allows you to use specific keywords that will place your book in front of readers interested in similar genres.

 Choose the right categories

Select less competitive categories where your book has a better chance of ranking higher. Amazon allows you to choose multiple categories, so pick one primary category and additional subcategories for more visibility.

 Free promotions

KDP Select allows you to run free promotions, which can boost rankings through volume sales and downloads. These can only be done within a ninety-day window, so be organised in order to maximise this opportunity. Any ebook that is downloaded during free promotion periods counts as a purchase, so the reader is able to leave a qualified review for you.

The Bestseller

Remember, sales will always slow down unless you are prepared to continue to promote the book and keep up the momentum. Stay engaged with your audience post-launch by continuing with your efforts on social media, email marketing and ads. Encourage readers to share your book, leave reviews, or participate in a book club or discussion related to your work. Get yourself out there as much as possible!

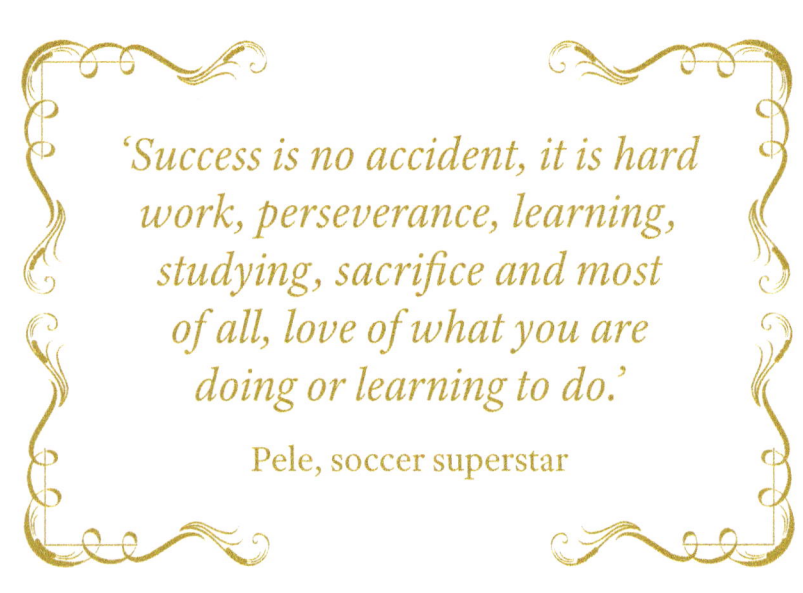

'Success is no accident, it is hard work, perseverance, learning, studying, sacrifice and most of all, love of what you are doing or learning to do.'

Pele, soccer superstar

The pep talk

Ignite & Write: The Published Author

If there's one thing I hope you carry with you as you close this book, it's this: there is no one right way to become a published author – only the path that's right for you.

Whether you dream of signing with a traditional publishing house, are building your brand through self-publishing, or find the perfect fit with publishing service providers, each route offers its own blend of challenges, rewards and creative milestones. There is no hierarchy here. Your story, your message and your voice matter, regardless of the publishing model you choose.

Publishing a book is an incredibly personal journey. It's equal parts strategic and soulful. It asks you to be brave, to be open and to trust in your message even when imposter syndrome creeps in. But the most powerful thing you can do throughout this process is to surround yourself with people who respect your vision and value your work as much as you do.

The publishing industry is vast, but not all services, professionals, or partnerships are created equal. So wherever your path leads, make sure it's lined with overhead lamps that illuminate support, integrity and creative alignment. If something doesn't feel right, you're allowed to pause. If someone doesn't treat your story with care, you're allowed to say no.

> When you find the right people who get it because they see your brilliance and want to help you shine, that's when the magic happens.

The pep talk

Remember, *The Published Author* isn't a title reserved for the lucky or the elite. It's for the persistent, the passionate and the purpose-driven. You've made it this far. You've dared to put your thoughts into words, to dream about holding your own book in your hands and to take the time to understand what it takes to get there.

So whatever you do next – whether you start pitching to publishers, finalise your manuscript for self-publishing, or launch your ebook to the world – do it with pride. Trust your instincts. Honour your message. Most of all, know that your words have the power to inspire, to connect, to heal and to ignite change.

You are not just writing a book; you are becoming *The Published Author*. Remember, you don't have to do it alone. At Ignite & Write, we specialise in guiding purpose-driven authors through every stage of the publishing journey, from refining your message to structuring your book and navigating the world of publishing.

Whether you're just starting out or preparing to share your manuscript with the world, our workshops, Author Amplifier membership and mentorship program and publishing support services are designed to meet you exactly where you are. We believe in your story, we honour your voice and we're here to walk beside you as you bring your book to life on your terms, with integrity and impact. If you're ready to take the next step, know that a passionate, experienced community is ready to welcome you.

It is incredibly exciting to see your book take on a life of its own once it's out in the world. It will land in hands and homes you've never seen, speak into hearts you'll never meet and start conversations you'll never overhear. That is the quiet, powerful legacy of authorship.

There may be days when the process feels overwhelming. That's normal. There may be setbacks, delays and detours. That's normal too. But every step you take is still progress. Every small win counts. Every brave action you take brings your book closer to the hands of someone who needs it.

So as you read this final note, take a breath. Reflect on how far you've come. Then, when you're ready, take the next step forward. The world is waiting for what only you can share.

Acknowledgments

At the launch of my first book, I stood on stage and boldly declared that I'd release book two within six months and book three six months after that. It was a confident plan and one I truly believed in at the time. But life, as beautifully unpredictable as it is, had other ideas.

There were lessons I still needed to learn, people I had yet to meet and industry wisdom that hadn't crossed my path yet. The universe already knew that, it just took me a little longer to catch up! What I've come to realise is this: it's not about how fast you finish, but that you keep showing up and honour the commitment you made to yourself.

So here we are, book three is in your hands. While it took longer than I imagined, I wouldn't change a single thing. Because sometimes, the best stories take time. When you do something as wild as announcing a trilogy before you've even written the first book, it takes a pretty special support crew to get you across the finish line.

While I may have written the words on these pages, they've been shaped, inspired and elevated by the many incredible people in my life. I have so many wonderful cheerleaders and amazing authors who have trusted me and become Ignite & Write alumni that I could easily fill a whole chapter with Oscar-worthy shoutouts. You know who you are! Thank you for being part of this ride. I value you more than words can say.

To Catherine and Martin, Gary and Sam and my in-laws Carol and Quentin, thank you for being the steady, grounding forces in my life. Your wisdom, warmth and unwavering encouragement have been a quiet strength behind everything I do. I'm deeply grateful to walk this path with such a supportive and loving circle of family.

To my wildly wonderful cheebies, Lilly and Lincoln, thank you for constantly reminding me how powerful imagination can be when it's left to run free. You are my daily inspiration, my proudest creations and the reason I keep chasing dreams with childlike wonder. Watching you express yourselves so boldly fills my heart in ways I never knew possible.

To my husband Chris, thank you for being the calm in the storm and the rock beneath our chaos. Your love, loyalty and deep belief in me make everything feel possible, even on the hardest days. I love you forever and a day.

To my soul-sister and editorial guardian, Candice Holznagel, your friendship has been a constant through so many seasons of life. You catch what I miss, challenge me when I doubt and always have my back. You make my words shine brighter, and I honestly don't know where I'd be without you.

Carren Smith, thank you for shaking me awake and reminding me what happens when you show up fully for your purpose. Your coaching cracked something open in me, and I've been walking taller ever since.

Acknowledgments

To Cara Ord, your talent is otherworldly. The artwork you've created for this series captures its soul in a way only you could.

Thank you Sylvie Blair for your design brilliance and precision. This book has your fingerprints all over it, and I couldn't be prouder of what we've created together.

Finally, thank you... yes, *you*. Thank you for trusting me to walk beside you on your authorship journey. It's an honour I don't take lightly. Keep showing up. Keep finishing what you start. Even if the road bends, even if life throws curveballs, know that it's all part of the unfolding. Stand tall, own your message and make the difference you were born to make.

About Roxy

Since 2007, Roxanne's unique and multi-award-winning method of storytelling has changed the lives of thousands of budding authors, allowing them to bring their messages to life in nonfiction books with structure, connection to the reader and potential profit.

A prolific ghostwriter, author, workshop facilitator, writing mentor and journalist, Roxanne's presentations are charged with powerful content and tangible tools that remove the mystery from storytelling and ignite a thought-provoking and emotion-evoking theatre within the mind.

Her *Ignite & Write* series has become a powerful resource for aspiring authors around the world to craft their manuscripts with confidence, clarity and a true sense of purpose and passion.

As an MC, presenter and speaker, Roxanne's down-to-earth, relatable, humorous style engages her audience, inspires their minds and moves them to begin to think laterally about their own stories and how their lived experiences and knowledge journeys can have a greater impact on the world around them.

Her emphasis on connection to her authors and honouring the uniqueness of their stories has seen her recognised in:

Ignite & Write: The Published Author

2024

- Sunshine Coast Business Awards Creative Industries finalist

2023

- WINNER Sunshine Coast Business Awards Creative Industries
- WINNER ROAR Awards Best Writer/Author Silver
- WINNER International Reader Views

2022

- Sunshine Coast Business Awards Creative Industries finalist

2021

- WINNER Micro/Small Business Woman of the Year, Sunshine Coast Business Women's Network Awards
- Australian Small Business Champion Awards Sole Trader Finalist

2020

- Australian Small Business Champion Awards Sole Trader Finalist
- Australian My Business Awards for Young Leader of the Year Finalist (one of only two female finalists)
- Australian My Business Awards for B2C Business of the Year Finalist

About Roxy

2019

- Young Business Woman of the Year Finalist, Sunshine Coast Business Women's Network Awards
- Australian My Business Awards Young Leader of the Year Finalist

Roxanne is a member of the Australian Society of Authors, Queensland Writer's Centre and Life Stories Australia. In 2021, Roxanne was recognised as an ambassador for No More Fake Smiles, a charity that provides advocacy and therapy for victims of child sexual abuse and their families.

To connect with Roxanne, visit www.igniteandwrite.com

References

1. Roxanne McCarty-O'Kane, *The Mindful Author*, 2022.

2. Joab Jackson, *Google: 129 million different books have been published.* PC World, August 6, 2010. Retrieved on August 7, 2024 from https://www.pcworld.com/article/508405/google_129_million_different_books_have_been_published.html

3. Talon Homer, *How many books are there in the world?* How Stuff Works, October 12, 2022. Retrieved on August 7, 2024 from https://entertainment.howstuffworks.com/arts/literature/how-many-books.htm

4. Val Giordano, *How many books are there in the world? (2024)* ISBNDB, October 20, 2023. Retrieved on August 7, 2024 from https://isbndb.com/blog/how-many-books-are-in-the-world/

5. Michelle Starr, *Can Our Brains Really Read Jumbled Words as Long as The First And Last Letters Are Correct?* Science Alert, March 31, 2018. Retrieved on October 14, 2024 from https://www.sciencealert.com/word-jumble-meme-first-last-letters-cambridge-typoglycaemia

6. *What our eyes can't see, the brain fills in.* University News, April 5, 2011. University of Glasgow. Retrieved on July 27, 2025 from https://www.gla.ac.uk/news/archiveofnews/2011/april/headline_194655_en.html

7. *The History of Self Publishing.* Alliance of Independent Authors, May 28, 2012. Retrieved on August 7, 2024 from https://selfpublishingadvice.org/history-of-self-publishing/

8. Arthur Rivers, *How Stephen King almost threw away his most successful book.* Fully Booked, October 27, 2021. Retrieved on July 3, 2025 from https://fully-booked.ca/editorials/stephen-king-carrie-almost-threw-away/

9. Rachel Gillett, *How J.K. Rowling turned rejection into success*. Business Insider, July 30, 2016. Retrieved on July 2, 2025 from https://www.businessinsider.com/how-jk-rowling-turned-rejection-into-success-2016-7

10. Emily Temple, *The most rejected books of all time (Of the ones that were actually published)*, December 22, 2017. Retrieved on July 29, 2024 from https://lithub.com/the-most-rejected-books-of-all-time/

11. Steve Chawkins, *Robert Pirsig dies at 88; wrote counterculture classic 'Zen and the Art of Motorcycle Maintenance'*. Los Angeles Times, April 24, 2017.

12. Emily Temple, *The most rejected books of all time (of the ones that were eventually published.)* Lit Hub, December 22, 2017. Retrieved on July 3, 2025 from https://lithub.com/the-most-rejected-books-of-all-time/

13. Saisuman Revankar, *ebooks statistics by revenue, user, country, sales, genre and facts*. Coolest Gadgets, February 12, 2025. Retrieved on July 3, 2025 from https://coolest-gadgets.com/ebooks-statistics.

14. Michael Kozlowski, *ebook sales soared 16.8% in April 2024*. Good E Reader, June 17, 2024. Retrieved on September 3, 2025 from https://goodereader.com/blog/e-book-news/ebook-sales-soared-16-8-in-april-2024

15. Michael Kozlowski, *Audiobook sales are soaring in 2024 – audiobook statistics*. Good E Reader, January 5, 2025. Retrieved on July 9, 2025 from https://goodereader.com/blog/audiobooks/audiobook-sales-are-soaring-in-2024-audiobook-statistics

16. William Dietrich, *The writer's odds of success*. The HuffPost, March 4, 2013. Retrieved on September 21, 2024 from https://www.huffpost.com/entry/the-writers-odds-of-succe_b_2806611

17. Tom Wells, *What is the average time spent on a website in 2025? A deep dive into user engagement*. Marketing Scoop, November 26, 2023.

References

Retrieved on July 9, 2025 from https://www.marketingscoop.com/small-business/what-is-the-average-time-spent-on-a-website/

18. Kevin Kennedy, *Why blog? Statistics show the benefits.* Marketpath, retrieved on July 9, 2025 from https://www.marketpath.com/blog/why-blog-statistics-show-the-benefits

19. *9 Steps to Self Publishing on Amazon: A Comprehensive Guide for 2024.* The Book Designer. January 12, 2024. Retrieved on October 14, 2024 from https://www.thebookdesigner.com/amazon-self-publishing-facts-and-faqs/

20. *From reviews to revenue: How star ratings and review content influence purchase.* Power Reviews and Northwestern University. Retrieved on July 9, 2025 from https://spiegel.medill.northwestern.edu/wp-content/uploads/sites/2/2021/04/Online-Reviews-Whitepaper.pdf

The Ignite & Write Trilogy

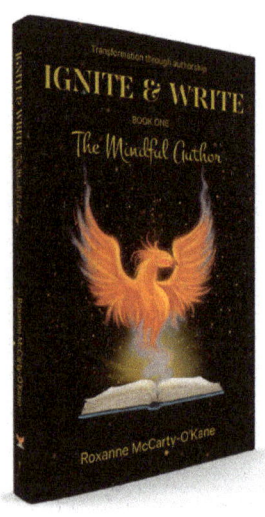

The Mindful Author

Winner of the International Reader Views Gold Award for Best Writing/Publishing Book and the Book By Book Pub Gold Award for Best Writing/Publishing Book in 2023. The first book in the *Ignite & Write* trilogy is a resource for you to find your inspiration and transform your fears, roadblocks and self-doubt into confidence and completion. It's time to embrace the mindset of an author and lay strong foundations for your writing success.

The Ignite & Write Trilogy

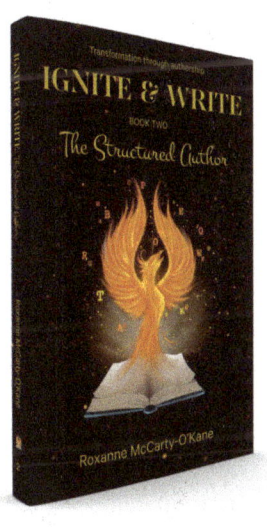

The Structured Author

Book Two in this series will take the guesswork out of *how* to write your book! You will be guided through how to draw all the thoughts, ideas and memories out of your mind and create a structure that contains every important element to keep your reader enthralled from start to end. It is also jam-packed full of information that will help you determine what style of book best suits your story and how to structure everything from the overall manuscript right down to the anatomy of a captivating chapter, so you can write with passion and purpose.

To experience the full Ignite & Write journey, complete the trilogy.
www.igniteandwrite.com

www.ingramcontent.com/pod-product-compliance
Lightning Source LLC
Chambersburg PA
CBHW062033290426
44109CB00026B/2616